CREATING A QUILTED HOME

25 Table Runners & Toppers to Make Each Day Joyful

by MISSOURI STAR QUILT CO.

MISSOURI STAR
QUILT CO.

EXECUTIVE EDITOR
Natalie Earnheart

CREATIVE TEAM
Jenny Doan, Natalie Earnheart, Misty Doan, Christine Ricks, Grant Flook, Mike Brunner, Lauren Dorton, Jennifer Dowling, Dustin Weant, Jessica Toye, Kimberly Forman, Denise Lane

EDITOR & COPYWRITER
Nichole Spravzoff, Liz Gubernatis

SEWIST TEAM
Jenny Doan, Natalie Earnheart, Misty Doan, Courtenay Hughes, Carol Henderson, Janice Richardson, Cathleen Tripp

ADDITIONAL PHOTOGRAPHY
Derek Israelsen Studio, Salt Lake City, UT

PRINTING COORDINATOR
Rob Stoebener

PRINTING SERVICES
Walsworth Print Group
803 South Missouri
Marceline, MO 64658

CONTACT US
Missouri Star Quilt Company
114 N Davis
Hamilton, MO 64644
888-571-1122
info@missouriquiltco.com

MISSOURI STAR
—— QUILT CO. ——

ARTICLES

SEW ALONG WITH MSQC!

Scan this code with your phone or device for Digital Extras!
(You will need to be connected to the internet to do this.)

1. Open your camera app.

2. Select the rear-facing camera in Photo mode. (No selfies here!)

3. Center the QR code to the right on your screen.

4. Hold your phone/device steady for a couple of seconds.

5. Tap the notification that pops up to open the link.

QUICK & EASY

TAKE YOUR TIME

COME GATHER AT OUR TABLE

Some of my favorite early memories with my family were when we gathered around our big, wooden farmhouse table (with all the leaves in!). It was a place for folding laundry, serving dinners, mending clothing, family games, homeschool science projects, special occasions, and so much more. One way I liked making birthdays and holidays even more memorable was adding a pretty table runner to our old, well-loved table. It immediately dressed it up and created a festive atmosphere in seconds. In life, it's the little things that make all the difference and while we may not have had the fanciest holiday smorgasbord or perfectly decorated birthday cakes, everything always seemed so warm and welcoming at our simple table.

This book is an invitation to come gather with us at our family table. We always have room for one more! No matter what the season or occasion may be, there's always something to celebrate. I try to find little things to make each day more special and even if it's just changing out the table topper and adding a new vase of flowers from my garden, it brings me joy. In this wonderful book, we've gathered together our favorite table runners and table toppers—plus a few brand new designs you'll only find here—for a total of 25 patterns! Just think of the possibilities. Transform your table, add appeal to your dresser, or a touch of flair to the end of your bed. Table toppers even work great as wall hangings. However you use them, they'll add a touch of personal style to your home.

You can make everyday extraordinary! Take your quilting talents to the next level and start decorating your home with these fast, fabulous table runner projects. We have a feeling you'll fall in love and soon you'll have a special table runner for any and every occasion you can imagine. They also make thoughtful gifts for housewarmings, weddings, anniversaries, and birthdays. From tiny houses to classic Missouri Stars, pretty pineapples and even cute candies, there are so many unique designs to choose from! And they can all be customized in any fabrics you choose. What will you create today? Come join me at the table and let's get started!

Jenny

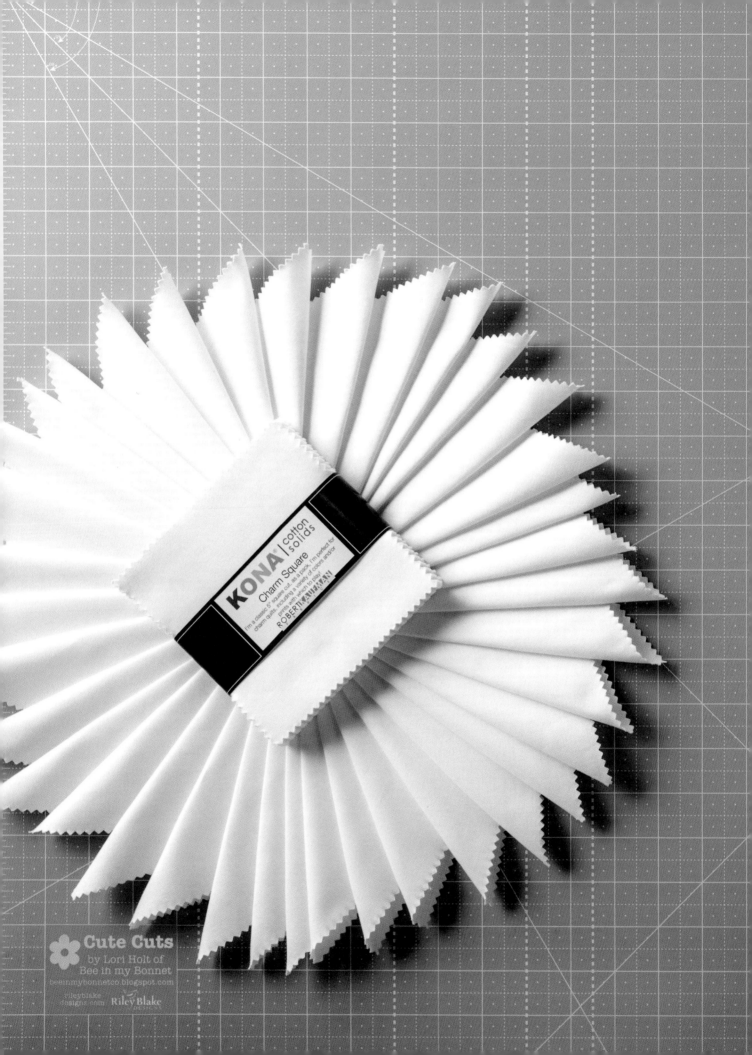

KONA cotton solids

Charm Square

I'm a classic 5" square cut, as a pack. I'm perfect for charm quilts, including a variety of colors and/or prints with which to play!

beeinmybonnetco.blogspot.com

ROBERT KAUFMAN

CREATING A TABLE RUNNER

Making a table runner from start to finish is a wonderful creative journey. I like to savor each step, from measuring and cutting to quilting and binding. There are learning opportunities throughout and while it can be a challenge for a first-time quilter to see how it all comes together, I assure you, it's entirely doable. Here are a few tips to help you on your way as you stitch up your beautiful quilted creation. I can't wait to see what you make!

CUTTING FABRIC

To get started, gather up your rotary cutter, ruler, and cutting mat. Remember your rotary cutter has a razor-sharp blade, so be careful and protect your fingers. Every time you're done cutting, make sure you close it up! And when the blade gets dull, change it right away so you can keep cutting smoothly.

Before you cut any fabric with a rotary cutter, put your cutting mat down to protect the table. It has a handy grid on it to help you line up your fabric as you cut. The ruler will help you as you cut your fabric. Line up your fabric with the ruler to get a nice straight line instead of using the grid on the cutting mat. Always cut away from yourself and keep your fingers far away from the blade using smooth, steady pressure.

SEWING

Once you have your fabrics cut, it's a good idea to change out your needle before you begin sewing. Use an 80/12 size universal needle. It's good for medium weight fabrics like quilting cotton. Also make sure you're using quality thread; 50wt cotton thread is great for piecing. Be sure to change your needle after about 8 hours of sewing.

If your machine has a foot with a ¼" seam guide, attach it to your machine to help you keep a consistent seam allowance. If you don't have one, use a piece of tape or a seam guide to stay on track, but don't be obsessed with perfection. It's more important to have a consistent seam allowance than a perfect ¼" seam. It will all work out in the end.

PRESSING SEAMS

As you sew blocks together, take care to keep your seams at a consistent ¼". Trim your blocks before you sew them together into rows. As you press your seam, when possible, press to the dark side. That way your darker seams will not show through lighter fabrics. As you create your rows of blocks, pay attention to which direction you are pressing the seams so that your seams will nest. Press one row of blocks one direction and then press the next row the opposite direction. As you sew the rows together, match up the seams, pin them, and then you'll find that they nest together neatly, creating less bulk.

When you're finished piecing your blocks together and it's time to add borders, please refer to the individual pattern for instructions to attach borders as placement may vary. Give your quilt top a good pressing with some starch or flattening spray. It's so much easier to work with a project top that isn't wonky and seams that lay nice and flat.

BACKING

Once you've pieced your beautiful project top, it's time to choose your backing! Measure the

length and width of your table runner top. Add an extra 4″ - 6″ to both the length and width of your quilt if it's going to be machine quilted. Trim off all selvages and use a ½″ seam allowance when piecing the backing.

As for quilting thread color, white, gray, or beige thread blends well with just about anything. Be sure to match your bobbin thread to your top thread. If you have any tension issues, using two different colored threads might result in a mess!

BINDING

The last step in creating your table runner is binding. Call me crazy, but I savor this part. I could easily stitch my binding on with a machine, but I love hand tacking my binding while I watch one of my favorite shows on the couch. It's just so cozy. You can create your own binding or you can buy it, but I often make binding from a jelly roll as it's already 2½″ and ready to go.

To make your binding, cut fabric straight across from edge to edge or width of the fabric. You can cut it on a 45° angle into 2½″ strips to create bias binding, which is recommended for curved or scalloped quilt edges. Sew your binding strips together with diagonal seams using the plus sign method. Press your joined binding strips in half and you're ready to sew your binding onto your quilt.

Finishing your very own project can be a pleasure. Taking the time to enjoy each step makes it even better. Instead of rushing through, find joy in your journey to the finished product. I often speak of quick and easy, and while that's true for many patterns, quilting is still a creative process to be enjoyed. It really does make a difference to thoughtfully finish a project. It takes your project to the next level and helps your quilt last longer as the years go by. I hope these tips help you create even more beautiful projects that will be treasured for a lifetime.

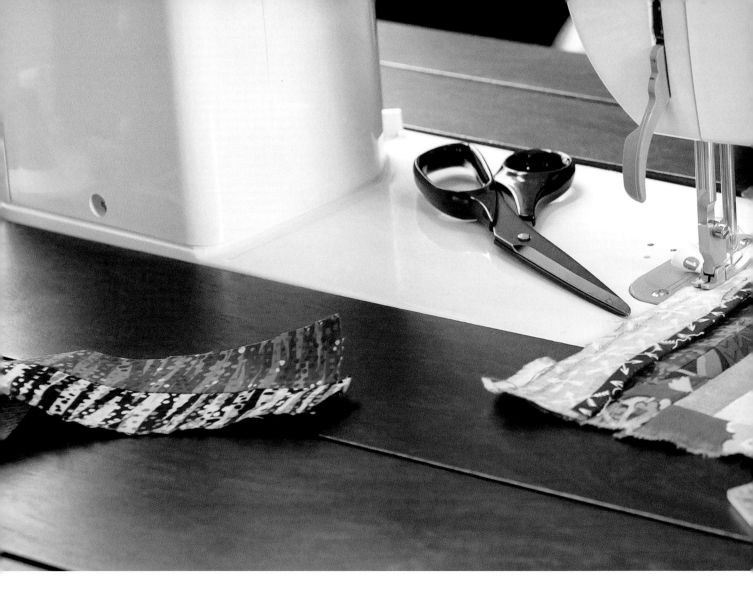

PRESS WELL

Before you layer your project sandwich together, it's important to press each layer of your project sandwich—even your batting! Everything needs to come together smoothly. It'll make quilting so much easier. And be sure your batting is right side up!

BASTE! BASTE! BASTE!

Pin the layers of your project together with safety pins every 2-3 inches so it doesn't shift as you stitch. Alternately, you can also spray baste your project sandwich together, but be sure to be in a well-ventilated area. Starting in the middle, spray a few inches at a time and work your way down to the bottom of your project, smoothing as you go. Then do the same on the opposite side.

MARK YOUR DESIGN

Using a hera marker, a chalk pen, or a washable fabric marker, mark your quilting pattern on your project so you can begin with confidence. If you aren't all about straight lines, skip this step for a more organic design that wibbles and wobbles a bit. Either way is beautiful!

USE A WALKING FOOT

Did your machine come with a walking foot? Awesome. If not, be sure to find one that works for your machine as all are a little different. It's a bigger, blocky foot with little teeth on the bottom. Without a walking foot, you will experience bunching and shifting as you quilt, so using one is essential. You will love the smooth results. The walking foot is so incredible because it helps to feed your fabric more evenly through your machine by working

with the feed dogs on your sewing machine. It's essentially a second set of feed dogs on top!

ADD THE EXTENSION TABLE

If your sewing machine setup includes an extension table, be sure to use it for an improved quilting experience. The extension table helps support your project so it can move freely under the needle without extra pull. And if your sewing machine is already dropped down into a sewing table, even better!

PUT ON QUILTING GLOVES

We recommend getting yourself a nice pair of grippy quilting gloves. They will help you control how your fabric moves through your sewing machine and you'll be able to maneuver your project with ease.

TAKE A TEST DRIVE

Before you take one single stitch in your beautiful project, make sure to test your machine quilting settings. That way you can be sure that your machine is feeding the fabric through evenly. It's much easier to do this than to rip seams! Check your stitch length, get familiar with the feel of your walking foot, pivot, try a curve, it's all up to you. Set your stitch length between 2.0 and 3.0, depending on the thickness of your thread, and get going! If you find that your stitches aren't as smooth as you'd like, switch out your needle and maybe your thread, too. If you're seeing whiskering or ripples in your fabric, adjust your presser foot pressure. Nothing can stop you now!

ADD A QUILTED TOUCH TO ANY OCCASION

Every season, or whenever I feel the whim, I like to change up the look of my table to compliment the flowers I just picked from my yard, a bowl of apples from the neighbor's overflowing tree, or anything that happens to be fresh that time of year. Whenever I design a table runner or topper, I try to plan a space in middle for a centerpiece. My patterns are designed to work in this way. I like to create a festive mood for special occasions like birthdays and anniversaries and over the years I've created a whole stack of table runners and toppers for each occasion. They all have special memories attached to them. Here are a few fun ideas to help you make the most of your home decor using table runners and table toppers.

ADD A CENTERPIECE

You may have noticed that my quilted table runner designs often have a space in the center that is just right for a big bowl of fresh fruit or pretty accents like a hand-picked bouquet of wildflowers, autumnal gourds in bright oranges or yellows, or a cluster of candles surrounded by greenery. This is a design feature I try to include as often as I can because table runners are meant to enhance your home decor.

MAKE COLOR COUNT

Think about the colors you often feature in your home and include hints of those in your runner, or even go neutral to allow your home decor to stand out. If you're undecided, try a double-sided table runner in two different color schemes, brighter and more subtle, to match the feel of your home at any given moment.

GO BEYOND THE TABLE

Runners and toppers don't have to be on a table. Try a longer table runner at the foot of your bed to refresh your decor without changing your bedding. Drape a table runner over a hall table or a dresser for a pop of much-needed color. Table toppers also make beautiful wall hangings.

PROTECT YOUR TABLE IN STYLE

By using an insulated batting for the center of a table runner or table topper, guess what? You have a great place to put a steaming hot casserole or an array of Thanksgiving sides without pulling out every hot pad you own! This has been especially helpful with our large holiday smorgasbord!

THE LONG & SHORT OF IT

Longer table runners that drape over the edge of the table create a more elegant look for special occasions. For less formal gatherings, it's completely okay for runners to be shorter than the length of the table.

MAKE A MATCHING SET

Create a quilt with a matching table runner or topper and your guests will do a double take! It's a great way to bring continuity into your home decor. Drape a quilt on the couch, add a coordinating runner on your table, and create a festive mood.

Creating a table runner when a special occasion arises is a quick way to make my home feel special. I don't have to spend hours and hours on it, and it gives me a feeling of accomplishment when I lay it on the table before my guests arrive. There's sure to be plenty of compliments and I am as proud of it as I am of the dinner I spent all day cooking! Taking time to celebrate with handmade touches helps make memories for years to come.

Fresh Strawberry Pie

One of our family's favorite summer treats is strawberry pie. I have fond memories of gathering around the table at the end of a long, sunny day spent outside in the garden. We would take only the best of the berries we picked to make this delicious pie. Add a generous dollop of whipped cream on top and it's absolute heaven!

INGREDIENTS

- Your favorite pie crust, baked
- 1 quart fresh strawberries
- 1 cup granulated sugar
- 3 tablespoons cornstarch
- ¾ cup cold water
- ½ cup heavy whipping cream
- 1 tablespoon sugar (*to sweeten the whipped cream*)

MAKING THE PIE

1. PREP & CUT
Take half of the fresh strawberries, trim off the stems, and slice them in half. Arrange them in a baked pie crust. Whisk together the cornstarch and cold water in a small bowl and set aside for later.

2. START THE FILLING
Mash the remaining strawberries and mix them with the sugar in a saucepan. Bring to a boil, stirring frequently until the fruit begins to soften and break down more, about 5 minutes.

3. FINISH THE FILLING
Gradually add the cornstarch mixture to your saucepan, reduce the heat, and stir until it thickens about 3 minutes, stirring frequently. Pour the mixture over the berries in the pie crust. Chill in the refrigerator overnight.

4. MAKE WHIPPED CREAM & SERVE
Whip the cold heavy whipping cream and sugar on medium-high speed until medium peaks form, about 3-4 minutes. Serve the pie with a dollop of sweetened whipped cream.

USING PRECUTS

Here at Missouri Star Quilt Company, we're all about making quilting and sewing easier and more accessible than ever before and precuts are the best thing since sliced bread! Precut fabrics are packages of fabric that are cut to size in advance. There's no need to cut fabrics for hours; they help you get right to the good part without all the fuss. Almost every single Missouri Star pattern is made to be used with precut fabrics so all you need to know is how many precuts to choose of each size and you're good to go!

Table runner projects are handpicked especially for precuts, along with a few tips and tricks to make sewing them together fast and fun. When you begin quilting with precut fabrics, it really couldn't be any easier. Keep on reading and learn how to make the most of each type of featured precut.

2½" PRECUT
JELLY ROLL

This is how we roll! Jelly rolls or 2½" strips are one of the most popular precuts out there for a reason. They look so cute all rolled up and they are incredibly useful. It's almost a shame to open them up for a project, but it's totally worth it. If you've ever spent a good amount of time trying to cut perfect strips, you know how valuable these rolls are! From log cabin quilts to sashing and binding, 2½" strips get the job done. You can even slice them up into mini charms and use them to snowball corners and add cornerstones. There are just so many uses for these simple strips!

5" PRECUT
CHARM PACK

Prepare to be charmed! Charm packs are so cute and so easy to use. We like to keep them on hand for quick projects. Gather up a whole bunch of them and before you know it, they're quickly used right up without a single regret. These wonderful stacks of 5" squares can be used as-is for easy patchwork quilts or you cut them up into neat little quilt blocks that couldn't be simpler to create.

10" PRECUT
LAYER CAKE

Layer cakes sound so delicious, don't they? These lovely stacks of fabric help big, beautiful quilts come together in a snap! Whenever we get our hands on one, they don't last long. We can't help but cut into them and get right to the good part—sewing! These fantastic 10" squares are perfect for quilters who are just starting out because of their versatility. You can do so much with a simple square. For example, you can make a quick set of eight half-square triangles with just two 10" squares. It's absolutely magical.

QUICK & EASY

These fast, fun projects are perfect for the rare moments when I get an afternoon all to myself! I gather up my sewing supplies, lock the door, and enjoy stitching to my heart's content! And by the time I'm all through, I can pop my beautiful, brand new runner on the table and order in some well-deserved takeout. These projects are also wonderful for last-minute gifts, seasonal decor (I am often guilty of sewing up until just before the guests arrive!), and are great for anytime you have that craving to create something quick and easy.

PERIWINKLE • HARD CANDY • FLIRTY • BORDERING TRIANGLE • CANDY TWIST • PONY EXPRESS • MINI TUMBLER • FLICKERING STARLIGHT • HEXAGON BRAID • FLOWER FANCY • MINI HOUSE

SEW ALONG WITH MSQC!

Scan this code with your phone or device for Digital Extras! *(You will need to be connected to the internet to do this.)*

1. Open your camera app.
2. Select the rear-facing camera in Photo mode. (No selfies here!)
3. Center the QR code to the right on your screen.
4. Hold your phone/device steady for a couple of seconds.
5. Tap the notification that pops up to open the link.

PERIWINKLE

Have you ever stumbled upon a treasure trove of antique quilts? We adore old quilts and making classic patchwork patterns part of our decorating for special occasions and even for random Tuesdays. This beloved Periwinkle design makes a gorgeous set of quilted coasters, chargers, and a table topper with a touch of vintage style. Savor old memories and make beautiful new ones with steaming mugs of cocoa, delicious hot dishes, and cool beverages. Make a few in different sizes for a practical and very pretty set of Periwinkles.

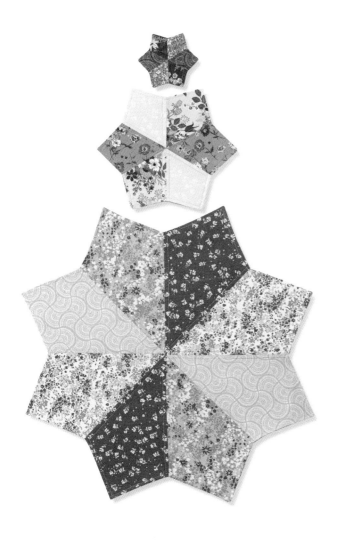

materials

PROJECT SIZES
Coaster - 4½" x 5½"
Small Topper - 10⅛" x 12"
Large Topper - 27" x 27"

PROJECT SUPPLIES
Coaster
(2-6) 5" print squares
1 fat quarter or 6" square
   of backing
6" square of fusible fleece
Missouri Star Mini Periwinkle
(Wacky Web) Template for
   2.5" Squares

Small Topper
(6) 5" print squares
1 fat quarter or 12" square
   of backing
12" square of fusible fleece
Missouri Star Small Periwinkle
(Wacky Web) Template for
   5" squares

Large Topper
(8) 10" print squares
1 yard of backing
1 yard of fusible fleece
Missouri Star Stretched Periwinkle
   Template for 10" Squares

2A

1 cut

When selecting your fabrics, the periwinkles can be all the same, from 2-4 different fabrics, or all different. You decide which look you are after!

For the coaster, use the mini periwinkle template to cut 6 periwinkles from 5″ squares. **Note**: As many as 4 mini periwinkles can be cut from (1) 5″ square.

For the small table topper, use the small periwinkle template to cut 6 periwinkles from (6) 5″ squares.

For the large table topper, use the stretched periwinkle template to cut 8 stretched periwinkles from (8) 10″ squares.

Cut the following from your backing fabric:

- For the coaster, cut (1) 6″ strip across the width of the fat quarter. Cut (1) 6″ square.

- For the small table topper, cut (1) 12″ strip across the width of the fat quarter. Cut (1) 12″ square.

- For the large table topper, cut (1) 27″ strip across the width of the fabric. Cut (1) 27″ square.

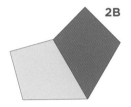

2B

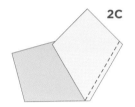

2C

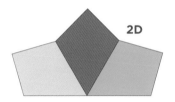

2D

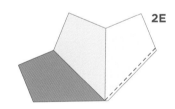

2E

2F

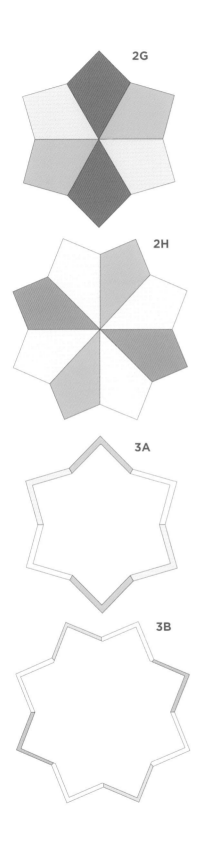

2 sew

Note: The coaster and small table topper each use 6 periwinkles. The large table topper takes 8 periwinkles.

Arrange the periwinkles with the tails all pointing to the center in the order you want them. Lay 2 different periwinkles right sides facing and sew along 1 side as shown. Open and press. **2A 2B**

In the same manner, add a third periwinkle. Press. **2C 2D**

For the large table topper only, add a fourth periwinkle. **2E 2F**

Make 2 halves for each project.

Sew 2 halves together as shown. Press these seams open. **2G 2H**

Tip: If your project doesn't lay flat, you can use starch and/or take in the seams towards the edges.

3 fuse

Lay the unit just sewn atop the bumpy side of your fleece and trace around the outside. Trim the shape from the fleece ¼″ inside the lines just drawn. Follow the manufacturer's instructions to fuse the fleece to the wrong side of the sewn unit. **3A 3B**

1 Arrange the periwinkles with the tails all pointing to the center in the order you want them. Lay 2 adjacent periwinkles right sides facing and sew along 1 side as shown. Open and press. In the same manner, add a third periwinkle. Press.

2 For the large table topper only, add a fourth periwinkle.

3 For the coaster and small table topper—sew 2 halves together as shown. Press these seams open.

4 For the large table topper—sew 2 halves together as shown. Press these seams open.

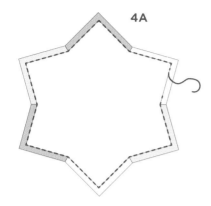

4A

4 add the backing

Place the top on the backing with right sides together and rough cut around it. Sew with the fusible fleece showing on top. Make sure to leave a 3" opening for turning along a straight edge. Begin and end by backstitching. **4A 4B**

5 finishing

Trim the back and clip the points and inside corners to reduce any extra bulk. Turn inside out, gently pushing the star points into shape. Turn the raw edges of the opening to the inside. Press. Topstitch around the perimter ⅛" from the edge to close the opening.

Quilt as desired and enjoy!

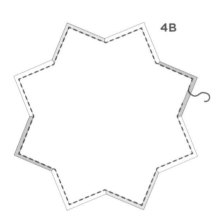

4B

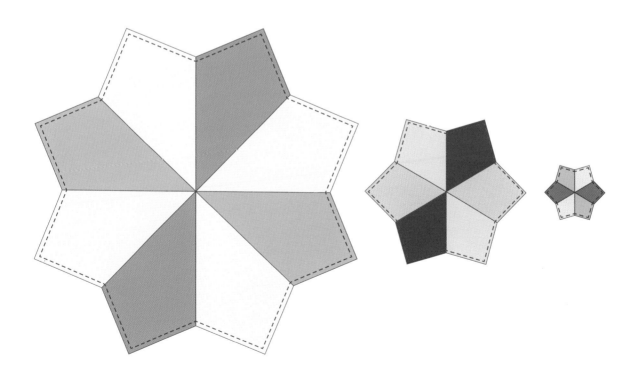

HARD CANDY

Grandmothers are known for having candy whenever the need arises. Just a quick dip into the depths of their deep purses and they can come up with a handful of different treats for all their favorite grandkids! But the sweetest thing is knowing that they're there for you whenever you need a hug or a listening ear. Take a moment to savor the sweeter things in life with a candy-colored table topper that's both pretty and playful. Made in a peppermint swirl of colors, it's as sweet as can be.

materials

PROJECT SIZE
24" circle

PROJECT TOP
(4) 10" print squares
(4) 10" background squares
(1) 5" background square for center

BIAS BINDING
1 yard

BACKING
¾ yard

ADDITIONAL SUPPLIES
Missouri Star Large Dresden Plate
   Template for 10" squares
(1) 4" square of fusible interfacing

1 cut

From the 10″ print squares, cut a **total of 10** fan blades. Align the template with the top of a 10″ square. Cut 1 blade, then flip the template 180° and cut a second blade. Each 10″ square will yield 3 blades. **1A**

From the background squares, cut 10 blades in the same manner as above.

Using a 3½″ circle template, cut 1 circle from both the 5″ background square and the 4″ fusible interfacing.

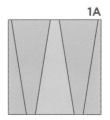

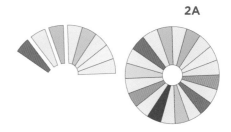

1 Cut 20 blades using the template. Arrange the blades in a circle, then sew them together and press.

2 Cut (2) 3½″ circles, 1 from print fabric and 1 from fusible interfacing. Lay the 2 circles together, the adhesive (bumpy) side of the interfacing circle facing the right side of the print fabric. Stitch around the perimeter of the circles. Cut a small slit in the interfacing and turn the circles right sides out. Use a pressing stick or small dowel to smooth out the curves. *Do not press!*

2B

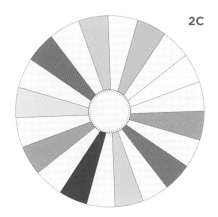

2C

CIRCLE TEMPLATE

2 sew

Sew the blades together, alternating a background blade with a print blade. After adding the last blade, close the last seam. **2A**

Lay the 3½" interfacing circle on the 3½" print circle, with the glue side of the interfacing touching the right side of the background square. Sew the pieces together by stitching ¼" inside the outer edge. Make a slit in the interfacing circle and turn the circles right side out. **2B**

Place the circle in the center of the blades. Press along the outside of the circle. Use a blanket or small zigzag stitch to appliqué the outer edge of the circle. **2C**

3 quilt

Layer the project with batting and backing, then quilt.

4 bias binding

Because the edge is round, you will need to make bias binding. From the binding fabric, cut a 34" square. Fold the square once on the diagonal. Press a crease in place along the diagonal fold. Place a ruler on the crease, and cut 2½" strips. Use the longest strips for your bias binding. You'll need enough strips to measure at least 76" after the strips have been sewn together. See page 47 for helpful hints on creating and attaching bias binding.

Refer to Creating a Table Runner (pgs. 10-15) for finishing and binding instructions. After the strips have been joined, gently press the strip in half with wrong sides together. Sew the binding to the front of the table topper, then fold to the back and whipstitch in place.

FLIRTY

We're enchanted by the sweet way just a few squares and a couple simple techniques turn into this Flirty table runner. Easy half square triangles and some simple snowballed corners create these patchwork hearts that steal ours! We turned our hearts so wherever you're sitting, you'll see our hearts flip and flutter for you. Setting your table with this charming runner, or sweetly dressing a front hall table to catch your mail and loving notes, we think you'll love it and you can stitch it up in a heartbeat!

materials

PROJECT SIZE
42" x 16"

BLOCK SIZE
9½" unfinished, 9" finished

PROJECT TOP
(12) 5" print squares
½ yard background fabric

BORDER & BINDING
¾ yard

BACKING
¾ yard

1 cut

From the background fabric, cut:

- (1) 5" strip across the width of the fabric. Subcut the strip into (6) 5" squares.

- (1) 2½" strip across the width of the fabric. Subcut the strip into (4) 2½" x 9½" rectangles.

- (1) 2¼" strip across the width of the fabric. Subcut the strip into (12) 2¼" squares.

2 sew

Fold each of the 5" background squares once on the diagonal with wrong sides together and press. Place a creased background square atop a 5" print square, right sides facing. Stitch on the creased line, then trim the excess fabric away ¼" from the sewn seam. Repeat for the remaining squares. Open and press. **Make 6** and set aside for the moment. We'll use these units for the bottom of the block. **2A**

Fold each of the 2¼" background squares once on the diagonal and press. Place a creased 2¼" background square on 1 corner of a 5" print square with right sides facing. Stitch on the creased line, then trim the excess fabric ¼" away from the sewn seam. Open and press. Repeat for the adjacent side of the square. Open and press. **Make 6** and set aside for the moment. We'll use these units when making the top of the block. **2B**

Lay out 2 bottom units and 2 top units. Sew the 2 top units together into a row and the 2 bottom units together into a row. Press rows in opposite directions. Sew the rows together and press to complete the block. **Make 3**. **2C**

Block Size: 9½" unfinished, 9" finished

2A

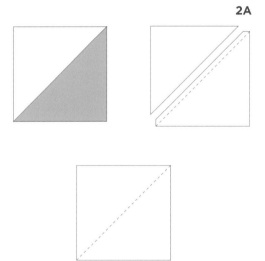

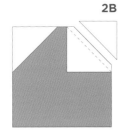

2B

3 arrange & sew

Refer to the diagram on page 45 to lay out the blocks in **1 row of 3**. Notice how the center block is rotated 180°. Add a 2½" x 9½" background rectangle between each block and to both ends. Sew the blocks and rectangles together to complete the center of the table runner. Press.

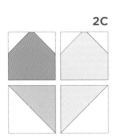

2C

1 Mark a sewing line on the reverse side of a 5″ background square. Place the background square atop a print square with right sides facing. Sew on the marked line.

2 Trim the excess fabric ¼″ away from the sewn seam.

3 Place a marked 2¼″ background square on 1 corner of a 5″ print square with right sides facing. Sew on the drawn line.

4 Add another 2¼″ square to the adjacent corner of the 5″ print square and sew in place. Trim the excess fabric away ¼″ from the sewn seam.

5 Press the unit. Make 2 for each block.

6 Arrange the 4 units as shown, then sew them together to complete 1 block.

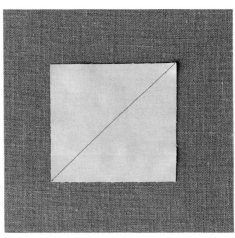

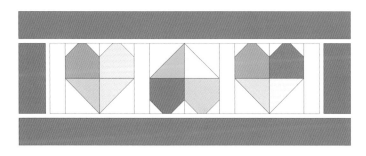

4 border

Cut (3) 4″ strips across the width of the border fabric. Sew the strips together to make 1 long strip. Trim the borders from this strip. Measure, cut, and attach the borders to the project top. The lengths are approximately 9½″ for the short sides and 42½″ for the long sides. Set the remainder of the fabric aside for the binding.

5 quilt & bind

Layer the table runner with batting and backing, then quilt. Refer to Creating a Table Runner (pgs. 10-15) for finishing and binding instructions.

NEW WAYS TO BIND A TABLE RUNNER

After hours of cutting, piecing, and quilting, it's time to add a beautiful binding to your project. It's so satisfying putting the final touches on something you made. The right binding can elevate your quilting. It's like the cherry on top! This final step brings the whole project together and there are more than a few different ways to get it done. To help you, we've gathered together a few more unique binding ideas right here. See traditional double fold binding instructions on page 13.

MATCHED OR PIECED BINDING

This special kind of binding has been carefully pieced to match the design on the project for color that flows all the way to the edge. It may look intimidating, but all it takes is a little extra work to create this clever modern binding.

As you sew the binding onto the project, you'll need to piece all the strips together by color, measuring them as you go to match the color blocks to the project top. To join one colored strip to a different color, begin by matching the first strip to a color block, then grab the second colored strip that comes next. Arrange the two strips so that they match their respective

color blocks and fold each strip back on itself where the two strips meet so you know where to sew them together.

Press the creases where the strips meet. Align the creases with the right sides facing and sew the strips together.

Trim, leaving ¼" seam allowance and press the seam open to reduce bulk. Repeat these steps where the color changes, stopping halfway to the next block. Pick up the next binding strip color, piece to the previous strip using the same technique as above, sew the binding to the project, and repeat all until all the binding is complete.

CURVED OR SCALLOPED BINDING

Dress up your project with beautiful scalloped binding. This type of binding is made from bias strips, because they have some extra flex, and that helps when you create a project with a curved edge.

To start, cut your 2½″ strips using the 45° mark on your ruler. Be sure to pay attention to the direction of your fabric if you have a print or a stripe and DO NOT cut on a fold. When you join your strips together, trim the ends square to help you line them up correctly.

Attaching bias to a curved edge can be tricky, but here are some ways to help it go smoothly. Be sure to measure accurately—don't just measure across the edge, follow the curve and go into the corners to get an accurate measurement to begin with. Start stitching a valley between the curves, don't start on a curved outer edge. Pin or use clips to keep your binding in place and don't pull it tight as you'll need flexibility.

Stitch slowly as you approach the valley and then, gently pull the quilt straight and stitch across, keeping your quarter inch seam intact. When you're finished, the curve springs back and forms a perfect little pleat. As you reach one of the four rounded corners, follow the curve and take your time. It'll turn out great! And when you go to stitch the binding down, guess what? There's no 45° angles to worry about at the corners, so it should all stitch down smoothly.

On Pins and Needles?

Do you ever poke yourself when finishing up your binding? Avoid the ouchies and use amazing Wonder Clips instead of pins to hold your binding in place while stitching. They're especially helpful with keeping corners nice and neat. You'll need about 50 for a table runner.

FLANGED BINDING

Add a little pizzazz to your quilt with a pretty flanged binding. This type of binding has a smaller strip in an accent color and it's easier than you might think to create!

To begin, cut 1½" strips for the main color of your binding. Then, cut strips for the accent color to 1¾".

Join the strips and press the seams open using the plus sign method. Cut a few inches off the main colored strip to offset the strips so that the seams don't line up and create unnecessary bulk. Sew the main color and accent color strips right sides together and press the center seam flat, being sure to press to the main color.

Finally, press your joined strips in half again and you'll notice that the accent color is peeking out beneath the main color. That's your flange! When you go to attach the flanged binding, you'll want to stitch it to the back side of your quilt first, with the front side of your binding facing the backing, and then fold it around to the front and stitch in the ditch between the two different fabrics to make your flange really pop.

FACING A PROJECT

This way of finishing a project may not be well-known to you, but it's pretty marvelous! This method eliminates the need for binding while preserving the edge of your project without interrupting the flow of the design. Facing a project with straight edges is similar to binding.

You simply cut double-fold binding strips equal to the length of each side of the project, but don't join them together.

Stitch each individual strip to the front of the project as usual, overlapping the top and bottom strips completely over the side strips (the side strips can be a bit shorter).

Once all of the strips are sewn onto the front of the project, flip them around to the back of the project and tuck the corners in, making sure the corners are still well-defined. Press the strips completely to the back and then stitch the bottom edge of your facing down onto your backing with an invisible ladder stitch.

Caught In a Tangle?

When hand stitching your binding, it's a good idea to use beeswax thread conditioner to avoid knots, especially if you like to use long strands of thread. Swipe it on the entire length of thread when you begin and it'll help you keep on stitching without breakage or tangles.

Give It the Slip

A slip stitch or ladder stitch is a great way to sew binding on. To begin, tie a knot in the end of your thread and pull it through the edge on the back side of your binding. Fold your binding over and put your needle back in right there, being careful not to go through the front of the project. Stitch to the left, through the middle layer about a quarter inch or so and poke your needle back up through the backing and the binding. Right where your thread comes out of the project, put your needle back down in and stitch to the left again, repeating the process. Your long stitches should be hidden inside the project and only a tiny bit of thread should be visible.

BORDERING TRIANGLE

Any way you slice it, a half-square triangle is a thing of beauty. For such a simple block, so many incredible designs can be created. Half-square triangles are in the majority of the quilts we make. They are one of the most versatile blocks in quilting, but don't let their simplicity fool you. When you turn and flip these blocks the design possibilities are endless! It's amazing to see what half-square triangles can become. This sassy table runner doesn't have to stay in the kitchen or the dining room. Hang it on a wall, decorate a dresser, drape it over a chair—enjoy your creation in any form!

materials

PROJECT SIZE
23" x 39"

BLOCK SIZE
4½" unfinished, 4" finished

PROJECT TOP
1 package 5" print squares

INNER BORDER
¼ yard

OUTER BORDER
½ yard

BINDING
½ yard

BACKING
1½ yards - horizontal seam(s)

1 Mark a diagonal line once on the reverse side of a 5″ light print square.

2 Place the marked square on top of a 5″ dark print square, right sides facing. Sew on both sides of the marked line with a ¼″ seam allowance, then cut on the marked line.

3 Open each section to reveal a half-square triangle unit. Square each to 4½″.

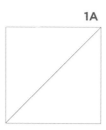

1A

1 sew

Draw a diagonal line once on the reverse side of (16) 5″ light print squares. **1A**

Layer a marked square atop a 5″ dark print square, right sides facing. Sew on both sides of the drawn line using a ¼″ seam allowance. Cut on the drawn line. Open to reveal 2 half-square triangles. Press the seam toward the darker fabric. Square each half-square triangle to 4½″. **Make 32**. **1B**

Block Size: 4½″ unfinished, 4″ finished

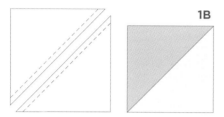

1B

2 arrange & sew

Refer to the diagram on the bottom left corner of this page to arrange the blocks in **8 rows of 4**. When you are satisfied with the arrangement, sew the blocks into rows. Press in opposite directions. Nest the seams and sew the rows together. Press.

3 inner border

From the inner border fabric, cut (3) 1½″ strips across the width of the fabric. Cut the borders from these strips. Measure, cut, and attach the borders to the project top. The strip lengths are approximately 16½″ for the short ends and 34½″ for the long sides. **Note**: The short ends are sewn on first, then the long sides.

4 outer border

From the outer border fabric, cut (3) 3″ strips across the width of the fabric. Cut the borders from these strips. Measure, cut, and attach the borders to the project top. The strip lengths are approximately 18½″ for the short ends and 39½″ for the long sides. **Note**: The short ends are sewn on first, then the long sides.

5 quilt & bind

Layer the project with batting and backing, then quilt. Refer to Creating a Table Runner (pgs. 10-15) for finishing and binding instructions.

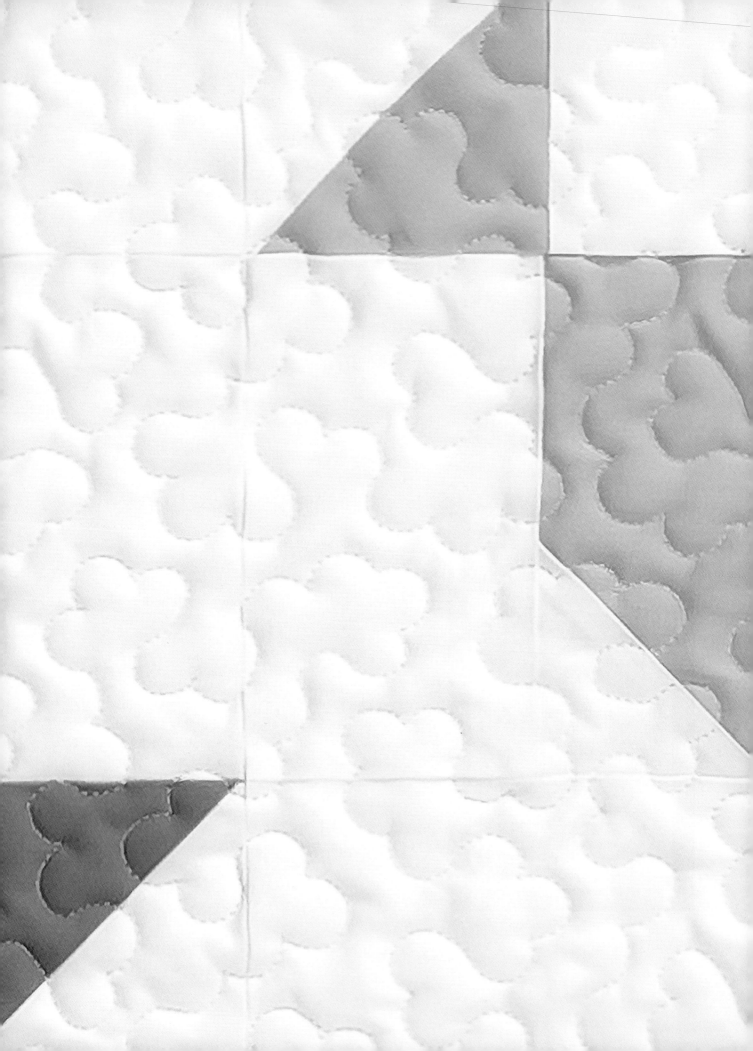

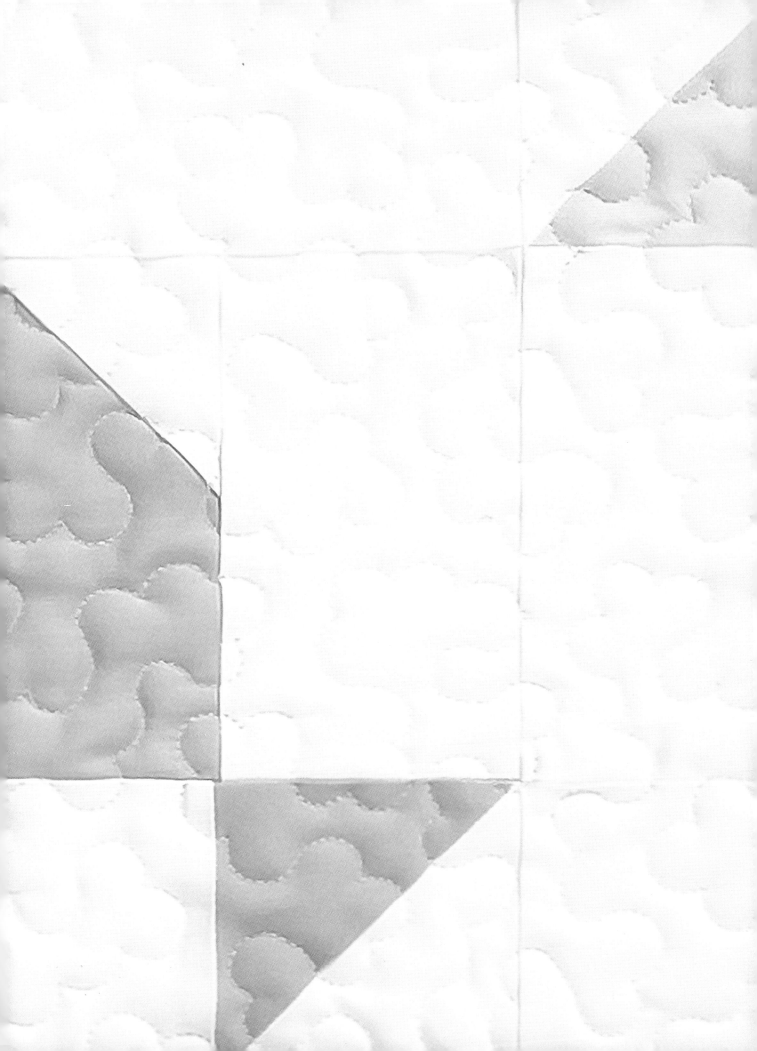

CANDY TWIST

Untwisting the crinkly wrapper from a sweet little piece of candy is such a treat. If you have a sweet tooth, this adorable Candy Twist Table Runner is for you. It's so easy to piece and can be made in fun and funky colors and prints for holidays, birthdays, and a halloween to remember! We left a space in the center for your bowl of candy or other sweet treats to take center stage. It's a fast, fun project that's sure to delight!

materials

PROJECT SIZE
9½" x 66½"

BLOCK SIZE
10" unfinished, 9½" finished

PROJECT TOP
6 pairs of matching 5"
    colorful squares
¾ yard background fabric

BINDING
(6) 2½" strips or (6) ¼ yard
    cuts of various
    coordinated fabrics

BACKING
1 yard - horizontal seam(s)

1 cut

From the background fabric, cut:

- (1) 10″ strip across the width of the fabric. Subcut (1) 10″ square from the strip and set aside to use as the center block in the runner.
  - From the remainder of the strip, cut (3) 3″ strips across the width. Subcut each strip into (4) 3″ x 7½″ rectangles for a **total of 12**.

- (1) 5″ strip across the width of the fabric. Subcut into (6) 5″ squares.

- (2) 3″ strips across the width of the fabric. Subcut 1 strip into (8) 3″ x 5″ rectangles and cut (4) 3″ x 5″ rectangles from the other strip for a **total of 12**.

- (1) 2½″ strip across the width of the fabric. Subcut into (12) 2½″ squares.

Cut (1) 2½″ strip across the width of each of the binding fabrics. Subcut (1) 2½″ x 26″ rectangle from each strip and set aside for the binding. Set the remaining fabric aside for another project.

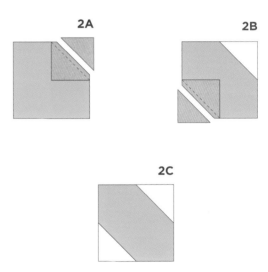

2 snowball the squares

On the reverse side of each 2½″ background square, mark a line once on the diagonal. Place a marked background square on the upper right corner of a 5″ colorful square. Sew on the drawn line, then trim the excess fabric away ¼″ from the sewn seam. Press. Repeat and sew another marked background square to the lower left corner. Trim as before. Press the seam allowances toward the darker fabric. **Make 6. 2A 2B 2C**

60

3A

3 make the half-square triangles

Layer a 5″ colorful square with a 5″ background square with right sides facing. Sew all the way around the perimeter using a ¼″ seam allowance. Cut the sewn squares twice on the diagonal. Open and press the seam allowance toward the darker fabric. Each set of sewn squares will yield 4 half-square triangles. You will use 2 of each set of half-square triangles. Set the remaining half-square triangles aside for another project. Trim each half-square triangle to 3″. **3A**

4A

4 block construction

Sew a 3″ x 5″ background rectangle to either side of a snowballed square. Press towards the rectangles. **4A**

4B

Pick up 2 half-square triangle units that match the snowballed square. Sew a half-square triangle unit to 1 end of a 3″ x 7½″ background rectangle as shown. Press towards the rectangle. **Make 2**. **4B**

4C

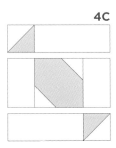

Sew the 3 units together as shown to complete the block. Press. **Make 6**. **4C**

Block Size: 10″ unfinished, 9½″ finished

1 Place a marked background square on the upper right corner of a 5″ colorful square. Sew on the drawn line, then trim the excess fabric away ¼″ from sewn seam. Repeat and sew another marked background square to the lower left corner. Trim as before.

2 Layer a 5″ background square with a 5″ colorful square. Sew around the perimeter using a ¼″ seam allowance. Cut the sewn squares from corner to corner twice on the diagonal. Open and press. Square up each half-square triangle unit to 3″

3 Sew a 3″ x 5″ background rectangle to either side of a snowballed square.

4 Sew a matching half-square triangle unit to 1 end of a 3″ x 7½″ background rectangle. Make 2.

5 Sew a rectangle unit to the top and bottom of the center unit as shown to complete the block. Make 42.

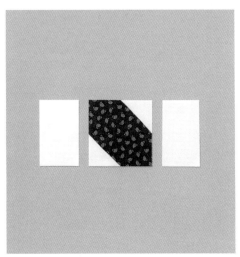
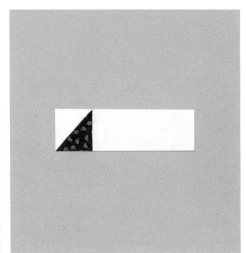

5 arrange & sew

Sew 3 blocks to either side of the 10" background square as shown on your left. Sew the blocks together. Press.

6 quilt & bind

Layer the project with batting and backing, then quilt. Refer to Creating a Table Runner (pgs. 10-15) and use the various rectangle units to add binding and finish your project.

PONY EXPRESS

Once upon a time, the fastest way to get packages across the country was by express pony! Starting in Missouri, delivery riders could travel 1900 miles to California, stopping every 10 miles for a fresh horse. Speedy delivery by horseback along a perilous prairie route, over the mountains and across valleys—can you imagine the adventures and stories Pony Express riders would have? We love seeing history woven into the fabric of quilting and this block was created in honor of their brave endeavors! Now you can enjoy it as a beautiful table runner.

materials

PROJECT SIZE
44" x 16"

BLOCK SIZE
12½" unfinished, 12" finished

PROJECT TOP
(5) 10" print squares*
¾ yard background fabric
   - includes sashing &
   border strips

BINDING
½ yard

BACKING
¾ yard - vertical seam(s)

*Note: (2) 10" squares need to match one another.

1 cut

Select the 3 non-matching 10" print squares and cut
(4) 2½" strips across the width of each square. Subcut
a **total of (48)** 2½" squares from the strips. Keep all
matching prints stacked together.

From the background fabric, cut:
- (1) 10" strip across the width of the fabric. Subcut the
  strip into (2) 10" squares. Cut (4) 2½" strips across the
  remainder of the strip. Subcut each of the strips into a
  (4) 2½" x 4½" rectangles for a **total of 16**.

- (1) 4½" strip across the width of the fabric. Subcut
  the strip into (3) 4½" squares and (8) 4½" x 2½"
  rectangles. Stack these rectangles with those already
  cut for a **total of 24**.

- (4) 2½" strips across the width of the fabric. Subcut
  a **total of (4)** 2½" x 12½" rectangles from the strips
  and set them aside for the sashing. Set the remaining
  background strips aside for the border.

2 make half-square triangle units

Mark 2 diagonal lines on the reverse side of (2) 10"
background squares. Layer a marked square with a 10"
print square, right sides facing. Sew on both sides of the
marked lines using a ¼" seam allowance. **2A**

Cut each sewn square in half vertically and horizontally,
then cut on the marked lines. Press. Each pair of sewn
squares will yield 8 half-square triangles. Square up
each half-square triangle unit to 4½". Set 4 half-square
triangles aside for another project. **2B 2C**

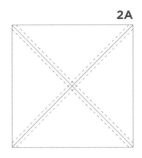

2A

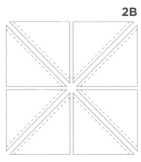

2B

2C

3A

3B

3C

3D

3E

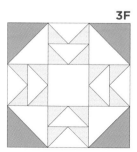

3 block construction

Mark a diagonal line on the reverse side of each 2½" print square. **3A**

Select 16 matching 2½" marked squares and (8) 2½" x 4½" background rectangles. Place a marked square on 1 corner of a background rectangle, right sides facing. Sew on the marked line. Trim the excess fabric away ¼" from the sewn seam. **3B**

Press open, then repeat with another 2½" marked square and snowball the adjacent corner rectangle unit to complete 1 flying geese unit. **3C**

Sew 2 flying geese units together. **Make 4**. **3D**

Arrange the 4 flying geese units, 4 half-square triangle units, and (1) 4½" background square in 3 rows of 3 as shown. **3E**

Sew the units together in rows. Press in opposite directions. Nest the seams and sew the rows together. Press. **Make 3** blocks. **3F**

Block Size: 12½" unfinished, 12" finished

3F

1 Draw a diagonal line twice on the reverse side of a background square. Layer it with a print square with right sides facing and sew on both sides of the drawn lines. Cut in half vertically and horizontally, then cut on the drawn lines.

2 Make flying geese units. Sew a marked 2½" print square to a background 2½" x 4½" rectangle with right sides facing. Sew on the marked line, then trim ¼" away from the sewn seam. Repeat for the adjacent corner.

3 Sew 2 flying geese together. Make 4 matching units per block.

4 Sew a half-square triangle unit to either side of a flying geese unit to make the top and bottom row of the block.

5 Sew a flying geese unit to either side of a 4½" background square to make the center row.

6 Sew the 3 rows together to complete the block.

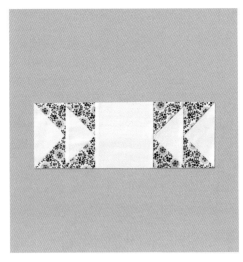

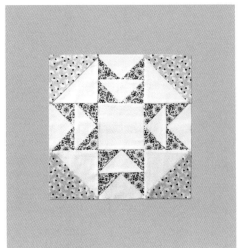

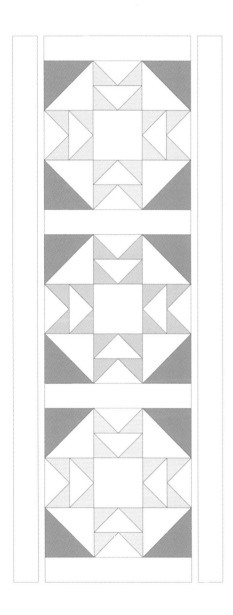

4 arrange & sew

Refer to the diagram on your left to arrange the blocks in **1 virtical row of 3.** Place a 2½" x 12½" sashing rectangle in between each block. Place a sashing rectangle at the beginning and end of the virtical row, then sew the blocks and sashing rectangles together. Press towards the sashing rectangles.

5 borders

Pick up the 2½" background strips you set aside earlier for the border. Sew them together to form a long strip. Measure, cut, and attach the borders to the long sides of the project top. The strip lengths are approximately 44½".

6 quilt & bind

Layer the project with batting and backing, then quilt. Refer to Creating a Table Runner (pgs. 10-15) for finishing and binding instructions.

MINI TUMBLER

A little tumbler cup with its gently sloped sides is such a fun shape—even for the angle-y challenged! Stitching these classic blocks together with the tiny peek of fabric overlap turns a topsy-turvy set of tumblers into a beautiful straight row! Always charming, they're lovely in reproduction or modern fabrics, scrappy or more planned out. We love how a few rows and a fun border make up this fast and easy runner in all our favorite colors.

materials

PROJECT SIZE
40½" x 20"

PROJECT TOP
1 package of 5" print squares or
    4 packages of 2½" print squares

BORDER
½ yard

BINDING
¼ yard

BACKING
1½ yards

ADDITIONAL SUPPLIES
Missouri Star Mini Tumbler
    Template for 2.5" squares

1 cut

If you are using 5″ squares, cut each square in half once to yield 2½″ x 5″ rectangles. Use the template to cut 2 tumbler shapes from each rectangle. If you are using the 2½″ squares, cut 1 tumbler shape from each square. A **total of 168** tumblers are needed.

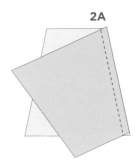

2A

2 arrange & sew

Refer to diagram **2B** below to lay out the tumblers in **7 rows of 24**. Notice how the every other tumbler is rotated 180° and the orientation of the tumblers are mirrored from 1 row to the next.

Sew the tumblers together to form the rows. Offset the tumblers by ¼″ as shown to create "dog ears" and use a ¼″ seam allowance to ensure the tumblers are aligned in a straight row. Press the seams of each row in opposite directions. **2A**

Sew the rows together, then press. Trim the ends of the tumbler even with the most narrow point of your rows, using a rotary cutter and ruler. **2B**

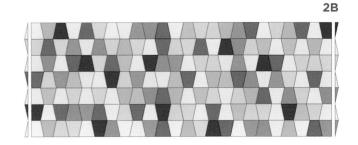

2B

3 border

Cut (3) 3½″ strips across the width of the border fabric. Sew the strips together to form 1 long strip. Cut the borders from this strip. Measure, cut, and attach the borders to the project top. The strip lengths are approximately 41″ for the top and bottom and 14½″ for the sides. Notice that the longer strips were sewn on first, then the shorter strips.

4 quilt & bind

Layer the project with batting and backing, then quilt. Refer to Creating a Table Runner (pgs. 10-15) for finishing and binding instructions.

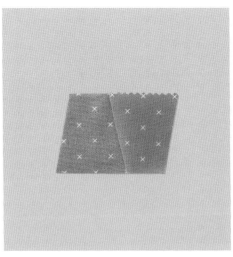

1 Arrange your tumblers in 7 rows of 24, then pick up the first 2 tumblers in a row. Place the second tumbler on top of the first, right sides facing and overhanging as shown. Sew the 2 tumblers together.

2 Open and press to 1 side.

3 Add the rest of the tumblers in the top row 1 at a time. Sew in the same manner and press all of the seams in row in the same direction. Make 7 rows and alternate the direction you press the seams for each row.

4 Sew the rows together and press. Trim the ends of the tumbler even with the most narrow point of your rows.

FLICKERING STARLIGHT

Camping in Missouri is pure bliss. It's dotted with picturesque state parks where locals flock every summer to relax, take a trail ride, go hiking, and sit around the campfire. There's nothing like a Missouri camping trip on a warm night. The crackle of the fire, a stream rushing nearby, and the hum of cicadas has got to be one of the best sounds in the entire world. This dazzling Flickering Starlight reversible table runner reminds us of those beautiful nights under the stars. It's the perfect accent for your tablescape. When you tire of one design, simply flip it over and enjoy another gorgeous pattern.

materials

PROJECT SIZE
20" x 52"

BLOCK SIZE
4½" unfinished, 4" finished

PROJECT SUPPLIES
(6) 10" accent squares for Side A
(6) 10" accent squares for Side B
2 yards black fabric-includes
   borders & binding

1 cut

From the black fabric, cut:

- (3) 10" strips across the width
  of the fabric. Subcut into (12) 10" squares.

- (8) 2½" strips across the width of the fabric for the
  Side A borders and binding.

- (4) 3½" strips across the width of the fabric for the
  Side B borders.

2 make the half-square triangles

Draw a line twice on the diagonal on the reverse side
of each Side A and Side B square. Lay a marked square
on a black square, right sides facing. Sew on both sides
of each line using a ¼" seam allowance. Cut each set of
sewn squares in half vertically and horizontally, then cut
on the drawn lines. Open and press each unit toward the
black fabric. Square each unit to 4½". Each set of sewn
squares will yield 8 half-square triangles and a **total of
48** are needed for each side of the table runner. Keep
the sets of half-square triangles for each side
grouped separately. **2A**

Block Size: 4½" unfinished, 4" finished

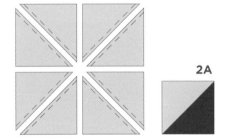

2A

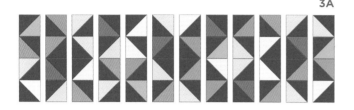

3A

3 make side A

Layout

Arrange the Side A half-square triangles in any pleasing manner of **12 columns of 4**. Sew the columns together and press the seams in opposite directions. **3A**

Nest the seams and sew the columns together to complete the table runner center.

Border

Sew (4) 2½" black strips together to make 1 long strip. Trim the borders from this strip.

Measure, cut, and attach the borders to Side A. The strips for Side A should be approximately 48½" for the long sides and 20½" for the short sides. **3B**

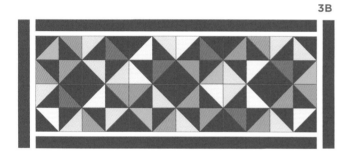

3B

4 make side B

Layout

Arrange the Side B half-square triangles in any pleasing manner of **12 columns of 4**. Sew the columns together and press the seams in opposite directions. **4A**

Nest the seams and sew the columns together to complete the table runner center.

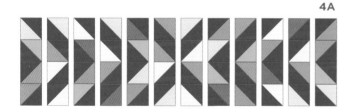

4A

Border

Sew the 3½" black strips together to make 1 long strip. Trim the borders from this strip. Measure, cut, and attach the borders to Side B. The strips for Side B should be approximately 48½" for the long sides and 22½" for the short sides. **4B**

Note: The 3½" border is to provide a wider back for quilting purposes. An even wider border can be added if you prefer.

4B

1 Mark a line twice on the diagonal of a 10″ print square.

2 Place a marked square on top of a 10″ black square, right sides facing. Sew on both sides of each marked line using a ¼″ seam allowance.

3 Cut the sewn squares in half horizontally, vertically, then on the marked lines.

4 Open and press. Each set of sewn squares will yield 8 half-square triangles. Trim each half-square triangle to 4½″.

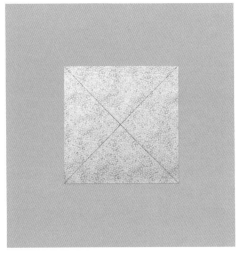
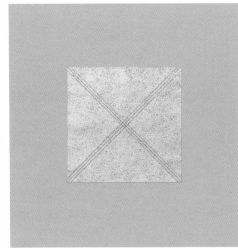

5 quilt & bind

Lay Side B right side down, and place the batting on top of it. Center Side A right side up on top of the batting. Baste and quilt as desired. After the quilting is complete, use Side A as a guide and trim away the excess batting and borders of Side B. Use the remaining 2½" black strips for binding to complete the project. Refer to Creating a Table Runner (pgs. 10-15) for binding instructions.

HEXAGON BRAID

We learned to make French braids, braids down the back, fishtail braids, braids that wound around or along the sides of the head, you name it! And when we started quilting, we loved learning to make this braided design, too! Just like a French braid, this pattern may seem complex, but it's so fun and easy once you see how it works. We're betting that when you get started, you won't want to stop. This pattern can be made as short or as long as your table and in so many colors you can have beautiful braids for every occasion!

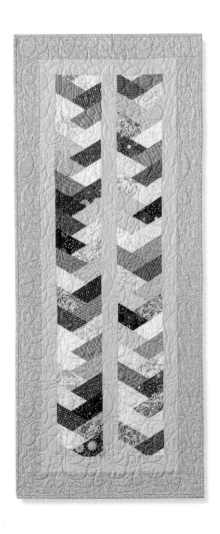

materials

PROJECT SIZE
23½" x 56½"

PROJECT TOP
1 package of 5" print squares
½ yard background fabric
   -includes sashing & inner border

OUTER BORDER
½ yard

BINDING
½ yard

BACKING
1¾ yards

OTHER
Missouri Star Small Half Hexagon
   Template for 5" squares

1 cut

Cut each 5″ print square in half once. Use the
template and cut a half-hexagon shape from
each 2½″ x 5″ rectangle.

2 make the braid columns

To begin a braid, lay 2 half-hexagons of different print
fabrics into position. The side of 1 half-hexagon will abut
the bottom of another. **2A**

Flip the bottom half-hexagon to the wrong side and
match the edges, leaving a dog ear at the beginning.
Sew the short seam. **2B**

From this point forward the bottom of the next
half-hexagon will always cross the seam just sewn.

Continue adding half-hexagons 1 after another until you
have a column with 21 half-hexagons along each side.
Make 2 braids. **2C**

Trim the short ends of both columns even. Measure ¼″
past the last point of the braid sewn into the column and
trim straight across as shown—approximately 46½″. **2D**

2A

2B

2C

2D

3A

3 sashing

From the background fabric, cut (5) 2½″ strips across the width of the fabric. Sew the strips together to form 1 long strip.

Measure the length of your columns and cut a sashing strip to the same length—approximately 46½″—from the long strip. Set the remainder of the long strip aside for the inner border.

Sew the sashing strip between the 2 braid columns and press. **3A**

4 inner border

Cut the inner borders from the long 2½″ strip set aside earlier. Measure, cut, and attach the borders to the project top. The strip lengths are approximately 46½″ for the sides and 18″ for the top and bottom.

1 Lay 2 half-hexagons in the position you'd like to start your braid.

2 Flip the bottom half-hexagon wrong side up and match the bottom edges. Let the bottom half-hexagon peek out under the top half-hexagon by ¼". Sew along the bottom edge of the top half-hexagon.

3 Fold the top unit back and press.

4 Repeat to add another half-hexagon to the top of the unit you just made.

5 Continue adding additional half-hexagon units to 1 side and then the other until you have made a braid that has 21 half-hexagons on each side. Make 2 braids.

6 Trim the short ends of both braids even. Measure ¼" past the last point sewn into the braid and trim straight across.

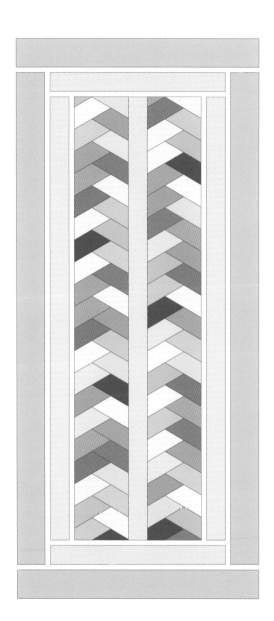

5 outer border

From the outer border fabric, cut (4) 3½″ strips across the width of the fabric. Sew the strips together to form 1 long strip. Cut the outer borders from this strip. Measure, cut, and attach the borders to the project top. The strip lengths are approximately 50½″ for the sides and 24″ for the top and bottom.

6 quilt & bind

Layer the project with batting and backing, then quilt. Refer to Creating a Table Runner (pgs. 10-15) for finishing and binding instructions.

FLOWER FANCY

Tumbler quilts have a special place in our hearts. They're one of our favorite vintage blocks! An antique tumbler quilt is like a time capsule—full of fabrics that remind us of why we made them, who we made them for. Setting the table for a fun tea party, brunch on the porch, or just a sunny afternoon, this runner adds a little special something that makes beautiful memories. This adorable Flower Fancy table runner was created with cute mini tumblers and it's a brand new way of looking at this traditional shape.

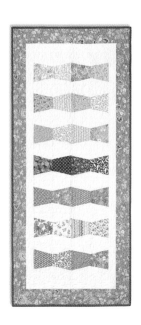

materials

PROJECT - CHARM SIZE
29" x 62"

PROJECT TOP
1 package of 5" print squares
1 yard of background fabric
  - includes inner border

OUTER BORDER
¾ yard

BINDING
½ yard*

BACKING
2 yards

OTHER
Missouri Star Small Tumbler
  Template for 5" squares

*Binding can be cut along
the length of the backing
fabric if desired.*

BONUS PATTERN

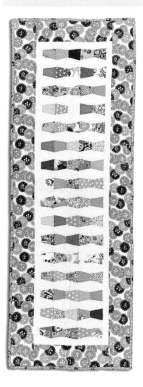

materials

PROJECT - MINI CHARM SIZE
19" x 58"

PROJECT TOP
2 packages of 2½"
  print squares
¾ yard of background fabric
  - includes inner border

OUTER BORDER
½ yard

BINDING
½ yard*

BACKING
1¾ yards

OTHER
Missouri Star Mini Tumbler
  Template for 2.5" squares

*Binding can be cut along
the length of the backing
fabric if desired.*

1 select & cut

Sort your 5" print squares into 7 sets of 4 squares of matching color. Set the remaining squares aside for another project.

Use the template to cut a **total of 28** tumblers from the squares. **1A**

From the background fabric, cut (4) 5" strips across the width. Use the template to subcut a **total of 32** tumblers, rotating the template after each cut. **1B**

2 arrange & sew

Refer to diagram **3A** as neccessary to arrange the tumblers in **4 rows of 15**. Begin with a background tumbler and alternate tumblers from the color groups. In the next row, set color groups in the same sequence, but flip them to match tops and bottoms of the previous row.

Select the first 2 tumblers of the first row. Lay the second tumbler atop the first, right sides together, and lining up the right edges. Make sure to create dog ears at the ¼" seam allowance. Sew the tumblers together using a ¼" seam allowance. **2A 2B**

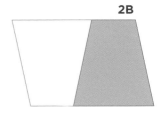

Continue adding tumblers to complete the row. **Make 4** rows and press in opposite directions.

Nest the seams and sew the rows together. Press.

3 trim

Place an acrylic ruler on the sides of your quilt top, connecting the inner part of the jagged sides. Trim the jagged edges of the sides of the quilt top so it is now a rectangle that measures approximately 51½" x 18½". **3A**

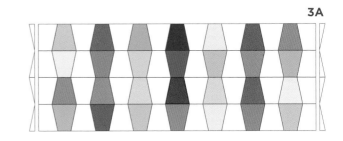

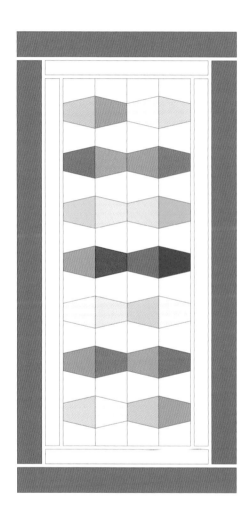

4 inner border

Cut (4) 2½" strips across the width of the background fabric. Sew the strips together to make 1 long strip. Trim the borders from this strip. Measure, cut, and attach the borders to the project top. The strips are approximately 51½" for the long sides and 22½" for the short sides.

5 outer border

Cut (5) 4" strips across the width of the outer border fabric. Sew the strips together to make 1 long strip. Trim the borders from this strip. Measure, cut, and attach the borders to the project top. The strips are approximately 55½" for the long sides and 29½" for the short sides.

6 quilt & bind

Layer the project with batting and backing, then quilt. Refer to Creating a Table Runner (pgs. 10-15) for finishing and binding instructions.

1 Use the template to cut tumblers from the remaining (28) 5″ print squares.

2 From the background fabric, cut (4) 5″ strips across the width of the fabric. Use the template to subcut 32 background tumblers. Flip the template after each cut.

3 Lay 1 tumbler atop another, as shown, with right sides together. Leave dog ears on either end. Sew along the adjoined edges using a ¼″ seam allowance.

4 Continue in this manner to add tumblers to complete a 15-tumbler row for the charm square project.

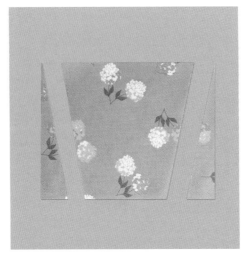

7 bonus mini charm runner

To make the Mini Tumbler Charm Table Runner, use 2½" squares and the Missouri Star Mini Tumbler Template.

From the print squares, cut 5 tumblers each of 16 print color groups for a **total of 80**.

From the background fabric, cut (5) 2½" strips. Subcut a **total of 85** background tumblers from the strips.

Refer to **7A** to arrange the tumblers in **5 rows of 33**. Follow the instructions in sections 2 and 3 to sew the tumblers together and trim the edges.

Measure, cut, and attach the borders to the project top.

For the inner border you will need (4) 1½" strips. Your inner border strips are approximately 49½" for the long sides and 12½" for the short sides.

For the outer border you will need (4) 4" strips. Your outer border strips are approximately 51½" for the long sides and 19½" for the short sides.

Layer the project with batting and backing, then quilt. Refer to Creating a Table Runner (pgs. 10-15) for finishing and binding instructions.

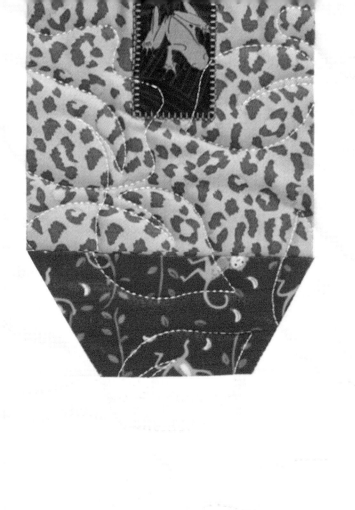

MINI HOUSE

Mormor is the Swedish word for "grandmother." There is something about going over the river and through the woods to grandmother's house that makes us all remember those comforts and anticipate that enveloping feeling of home. These sweet little houses make us feel right at home in this welcoming Mini House table runner. Cute houses all lined up in neat rows always welcome you to Mormor's neighborhood. It's a wonderful way to use our Small Half-Hexagon Template.

materials

PROJECT SIZE
42¾" x 17½"

PROJECT TOP
1 package of 5" print squares
½ yard background fabric

BINDING
½ yard

BACKING
1½ yards*

OTHER
Missouri Star Small Half Hexagon
   Template for 5" squares &
   2.5" strips
(2) 5" squares of Heat n Bond Lite

*__Note__: Depending on the exact size of your project, you may be able to use ¾ yard of backing fabric cut in half vertically, then pieced together with vertical seam(s).

1 fuse

Follow the manufacturer's instructions to apply the Heat n Bond squares to the reverse side of (2*) 5" print squares.

*Additional print squares can be used for variety if you like.

Cut each fused square in half vertically and horizontally to yield 2½" squares. Subcut each 2½" square in half again to yield 1¼" x 2½" door rectangles. A **total of 12** door rectangles will be needed and any extra can be set aside.

2 make the houses

Remove and discard the paper backing from a door rectangle. Place the door rectangle on top of a 5" print square as shown and follow the manufacturer's instructions to adhere it in place. **2A**

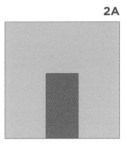

2A

Stitch around the edges of the fused door with a blanket or zigzag stitch to appliqué it in place. **Make 12** houses. **2B**

2B

3 make the streets

Cut (2) 2¾" strips across the width of the background fabric. Subcut a **total of (14)** 2¾" x 5" rectangles. Set the remainder of the fabric aside for now.

Arrange 6 houses in a row and place a 2¾" x 5" background rectangle in between each house and on the ends of the row. Sew the row together and press. **Make 2** rows.

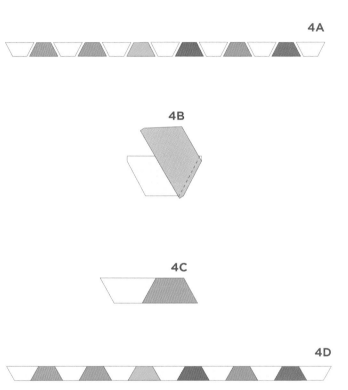

4A

4B

4C

4D

4 make the roofs & sky

Cut (1) 5″ strip across the width of the background fabric. Subcut a **total of (7)** 5″ squares for the sky. Set the remainder of the fabric and any scraps leftover from cutting the squares aside for now.

Select (6) 5″ print squares. Fold each square in half and align the short side of the template along the fold. Cut around the template. Each square will yield 2 half-hexagons and a **total of 12** are needed for the roofs.

Note: If your 5″ squares are a bit small, you may have to cut on the fold.

In the same manner, cut a **total of 14** half-hexagons from the 5″ background squares for the sky.

Alternate 7 background and 6 print half-hexagons and form a row as shown. **4A**

Tip: You might like to lay out your row of half-hexagons above each of your street rows to select the particular fabric you would like to use for the roof of each house.

Place 2 adjacent half-hexagons right sides facing and aligned as shown. Sew the half-hexagons together and press. **4B 4C**

Continue in the same manner to add the remaining half-hexagons until you have a completed row. Press. **Make 2** roof rows. **4D**

1 Remove and discard the paper backing from a 1¼" x 2½" door rectangle. Place the door on top of a 5" print square. Adhere the door in place according to the manufacturer's instructions.

2 Stitch around the edges of the fused door with a blanket or zigzag stitch to appliqué it in place. Make 12 houses.

3 Lay a print half-hexagon on top of a background half-hexagon, right sides together. Match the edges as shown. Sew along the matched edge.

4 Fold the top unit back and press.

5 Continue adding half-hexagons until you have sewn a row of 7 background and 6 print half-hexagons. Press after sewing on each new unit. Make 2 roof rows.

6 Finger press the center of a house row and a roof row. Match the centers, then sew the roof row to the house row. Press. Trim the ends of the roof row even with the ends of the house row it is attached to.

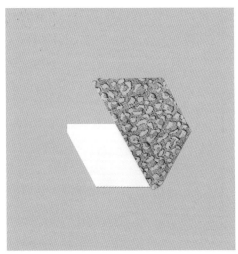

5A

5B

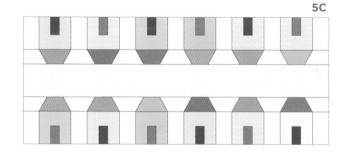

5C

5 table runner assembly

Fold each roof row in half and finger press to mark the center. Repeat to mark the center of each house row.

Align the finger pressed centers of 1 roof row and 1 house row. The roof row will overhang each end of the house row. Pin in place as needed. Sew 2 rows together and press. **Make 2**. **5A**

Trim the excess roof row even with the house row. **5B**

Measure the rows. They should be approximately 43¼" long. Cut a 5" strip across the width of the background fabric. Trim the strip to the same width as your rows.

Note: If your rows are wider than your fabric, use the leftover fabric from section 3 to piece together a strip that is the same width as your row.

Sew a row to each side of the 5" background strip you just cut. Press. **5C**

6 quilt & bind

Layer your project with batting and backing, then quilt. Refer to Creating a Table Runner (pgs. 10-15) for finishing and binding instructions.

TAKE YOUR TIME

Ease into these slow and steady projects when you want to savor each stitch. There's a time for quick and easy, but there's also a time to pace yourself. For me, hand stitching is a peaceful practice that lends itself to long winters spent by the fireplace, quiet nights in, and serene mornings. In fact, when life speeds up is exactly when I want a slower project. They are meditative and relaxing, the perfect antidote for a busy day. Hand stitching is also great when you want to take a project on the go. Tuck a few appliquè blocks into your purse and stitch anytime you have a spare moment.

DRESDEN SUNBURST • CHARMED SPOOLS • MINI MISSOURI STAR • DRESDEN SUNRISE • LOVE IS IN THE AIR • EASY CATHEDRAL WINDOW • SUMMER NIGHTS • FRIENDSHIP • FANCY FAN • JENNY'S DOLL • LEAFY TREE TOPS • TROPICAL PARADISE • GRANDMA MAE'S ECONOMY BLOCK • FLOWER CHAIN

SEW ALONG WITH MSQC!

Scan this code with your phone or device for Digital Extras!
(You will need to be connected to the internet to do this.)

1. Open your camera app.
2. Select the rear-facing camera in Photo mode. (No selfies here!)
3. Center the QR code to the right on your screen.
4. Hold your phone/device steady for a couple of seconds.
5. Tap the notification that pops up to open the link.

DRESDEN SUNBURST

Capture a sense of sunlight, summer, and glow with the Dresden Starburst pattern. This table topper looks just as good on the wall as on the table in the hall. Once upon a time, this classic was always made with pastel floral feed sack glory. Let the sunlight in with this fresh new version of the beautiful Dresden plate in a table topper that's just bursting with color! By cleverly folding white charm squares and inserting them between the blades of the Dresden plate, you can add a brilliant spark to this beloved traditional pattern.

materials

PROJECT SIZE
30" x 30"

PROJECT TOP
1 package of 10" print squares*
1 yard background fabric

OUTER BORDER
½ yard

BINDING
½ yard

BACKING
1 yard

OTHER
Missouri Star Large Dresden Plate
  Template for 10" Squares
Missouri Star Small Simple Wedge
  Template for 5" squares
5" square of Heat n Bond Lite

***Note:** You can substitue (9) 10"
print squares for the package if
you wish. More squares can be
used for added variety.*

1 select & cut

Select at least (7) 10" print squares from your package. Use the Dresden template to cut a **total of 20** blades from the squares. **1A**

From the background fabric:
- Cut (1) 24½" strip across the width of the fabric. Subcut (1) 24½" square.

- Cut (1) 4½" strip across the width of the fabric. Subcut a **total of 20** wedges from the strip using the wedge template. **1B**

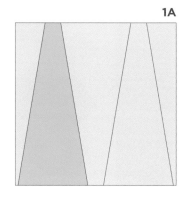

1A

2 prepare blades

Fold each blade in half lengthwise with right side facing. Stitch a ¼" seam across the wide end—chain piecing will speed things up. Trim the corner and turn right side out. Center the seam in the back and press to finish. **2A 2B 2C**

1B

3 make a sunburst

Fold a background wedge in half wrong sides together and press. **3A**

Pair 2 Dresden blades right sides facing. Sandwich a folded wedge between them matching all raw edges. The pointed tip of the simple wedge faces upwards. **3B**

Stitch the Dresdens together along, capturing the wedge in the seam. **3C**

Continue sewing blades together in this fashion, each time inserting a small wedge into the seam until you have formed a circle of 20 Dresden blades. Press flat with all of the wedges laying in the same direction.

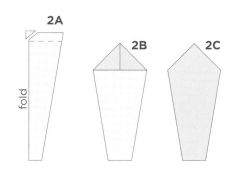

2A

fold

2B

2C

4 appliqué

Fold the 24½″ background square in half both vertically and horizontally and lightly press creases to indicate the center. Use the creases as guidelines to position the Dresden plate onto the background square. Pin in place as needed.

Trace a 4″ circle in pencil onto (2) 10″ print squares. Cut around each, adding ¼″ all around. **4A**

Sew the circles together with right sides facing on the 4″ marked line. Trim the seam allowance. Turn by pulling the fabrics apart and cut a slit in 1 side only. Make it large enough to turn the circle right side out. **4B**

Smooth the seam and press.

Following the manufacturer's instructions, use a small piece of fusible web to adhere the circle onto the center of the sunburst. Be sure all raw edges of the folded wedges are covered by the circle. Machine appliqué around the circle using a blanket, straight, or zigzag stitch, then using the same stitch, machine appliqué around the folded wedges. **Tip**: Use the "needle down" feature on your machine, if it has it.

Once the center is attached, appliqué the outer blades to the background square. **4C**

3A

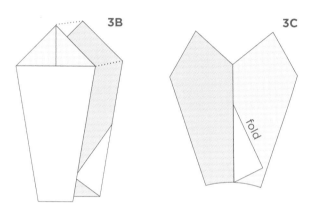

3B   3C

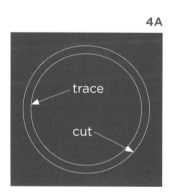

4A

trace

cut

4″ CIRCLE TEMPLATE

1 Use the template to cut 20 blades from the 10″ squares.

2 Fold each plate in half lengthwise, press and stitch across the top using ¼″ seam allowance.

3 Turn each blade right side out and press.

4 Fold the simple wedges in half with wrong sides together and press.

5 Sandwich a folded wedge between each blade with the point facing upward and stitch the pieces together.

6 Open and press all wedges so they are going in the same direction.

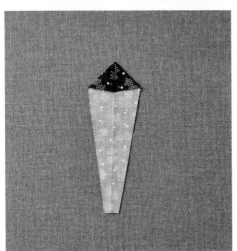

4B

4C

5 border

From the border fabric, cut (3) 3½″ strips across the width of the fabric. Sew the strips together to form 1 long strip. Cut the borders from this strip. Measure, cut, and attach the borders to the project top. The strip lengths are approximately 24½″ for the sides and 30½″ for the top and bottom.

6 quilt & bind

Layer the project with batting and backing, then quilt. Refer to Creating a Table Runner (pgs. 10-15) for finishing and binding instructions.

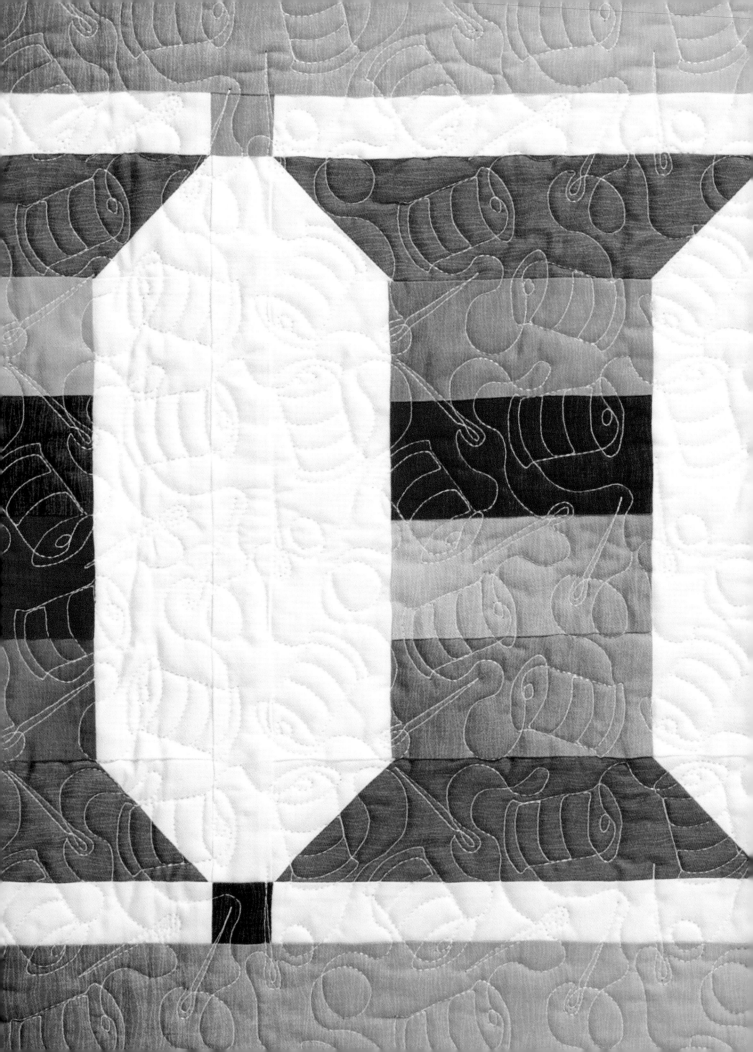

CHARMED SPOOLS

Fabric is often the star of the show on any of our projects, but we wouldn't want to forget to celebrate all the gorgeous threads that shine, too! This Charmed Spools runner builds four beautiful spool blocks lined up all neatly in a row. We love how varying the colors makes these spools look like luscious variegated threads. It also stitches up in your favorite fun colors—stack similar shades to inspire your inner seamstress and celebrate spools of creativity.

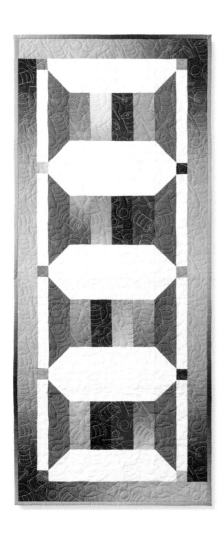

materials

PROJECT SIZE
43" x 18"

BLOCK SIZE
9" x 12½" unfinished,
8½" x 12" finished

PROJECT TOP
1 package of 5" print squares
   - includes cornerstones
½ yard of background fabric
   - includes sashing
1½ yards accent fabric
   - includes backing

BORDER
¼ yard

BINDING
½ yard

1 cut

From the accent fabric, cut (2) 2½" strips *along the length* of the fabric. Subcut a **total of (8)** 2½" x 9" rectangles from the strips. Set the remaining fabric aside for the backing.

From the background fabric, cut (3) 2½" strips *across the width* of the fabric. Set the remaining fabric aside for now.

- From 2 strips, subcut a **total of (8)** 2½" x 8½" rectangles.

- From 1 strip, subcut a **total of (16)** 2½" squares.

2 sew thread units

2A

Lay 2 different 5" print squares right sides together. Sew along 2 opposite sides of the stacked squares. Cut the stacked squares in the center, parallel to the sewn seams. Press. **Make 8**. **2A 2B**

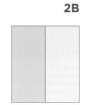

2B

Lay 2 units together, right sides facing. Sew them together to form a row as shown. Press. **Make 4**. **2C**

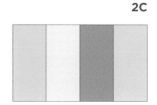

2C

Rotate each row 90°, then sew a 2½" x 8½" background rectangle to each long side as shown. Press. **Make 4** thread units and set them aside for now. **2D**

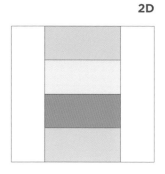

2D

3 sew spool units

Mark a diagonal line on the reverse side of each 2½" background square. **3A**

Place a marked square on each end of a 2½" x 9" accent rectangle as shown. Sew on the marked lines, then trim the excess fabric ¼" away from the sewn seams. Press. **Make 8** spool units. **3B 3C 3D**

3A

3B

3C

3D

4 block construction

Sew a spool unit to the top and bottom of a thread unit as shown. Press. **Make 4**. **4A**

Block Size: 9″ x 12½″ unfinished, 8½″ x 12″ unfinished

5 arrange & sew

From a variety of 5″ print squares, cut at least (1) 1½″ strip across the width of each square. Subcut a **total of (10)** 1½″ cornerstone squares from the strips.

Note: Each 5″ square can yield up to (9) 1½″ squares. At least (2) 5″ squares are needed, but more can be used for added variety.

From the background fabric, cut (4) 1½″ strips across the width of the fabric.

- From 2 of the strips, subcut a **total of (5)** 1½″ x 12½″ rectangles.

- From 2 of the strips, subcut a **total of (8)** 1½″ x 9″ rectangles.

4A

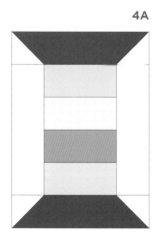

Arrange the blocks in **1 row of 4**. Place a 1½″ x 12½″ background rectangle between the blocks and on each end. Sew the blocks and rectangles together to form a row. Press. Set aside for a moment.

Sew (5) 1½″ cornerstone squares and (4) 1½″ x 9″ background rectangles together end-to-end to form a row. **Make 2**. **5A**

Sew the 3 rows you have made together as shown in the diagram on page 127. Press.

1 Place (2) 5″ print squares right sides together. Sew along 2 opposite sides of the stacked squares. Cut the stacked squares in the center, parallel to the sewn seams.

2 Open and press. Make 8 units.

3 Sew 2 unmatching units together. Press. Sew a 2½″ x 8½″ background rectangle to each long side of the unit. Make 4 thread units.

4 Place a marked background square on each end of a 2½″ x 9″ accent rectangle as shown. Sew on the marked line, then trim the excess fabric.

5 Press. Make 8 spool units.

6 Sew a spool unit to the top and bottom of each thread unit. Pay close attention to the orientation of the spool units.

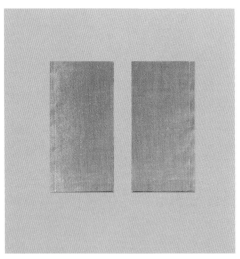

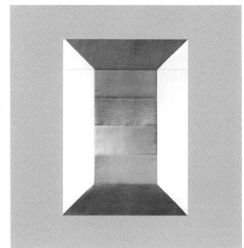

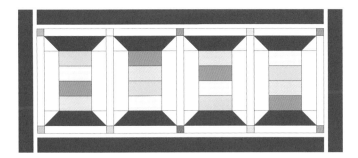

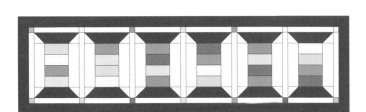

6 border

From the border fabric, cut (3) 2½" strips across the width of the fabric. Cut the outer borders from these strips. Measure, cut, and attach the borders to the project top. The strip lengths are approximately 39½" for the top and bottom and 18½" for the sides. Notice that the top and bottom borders are sewn on first, then the short ends.

7 quilt & bind

Layer the project with batting and backing, then quilt. Refer to Creating a Table Runner (pgs. 10-15) for finishing and binding instructions.

8 bonus

You can easily make this table runner longer! To make the 62" x 18" table runner shown in the diagram on your left, cut (12) 2½" x 9" accent rectangles, (24) 2½" background squares, (7) 1½" x 12½" sashing rectangles, (12) 1½" x 9" sashing rectangles, and (14) 1½" cornerstone squares. **Make 6** blocks using at least (12) 5" print squares.

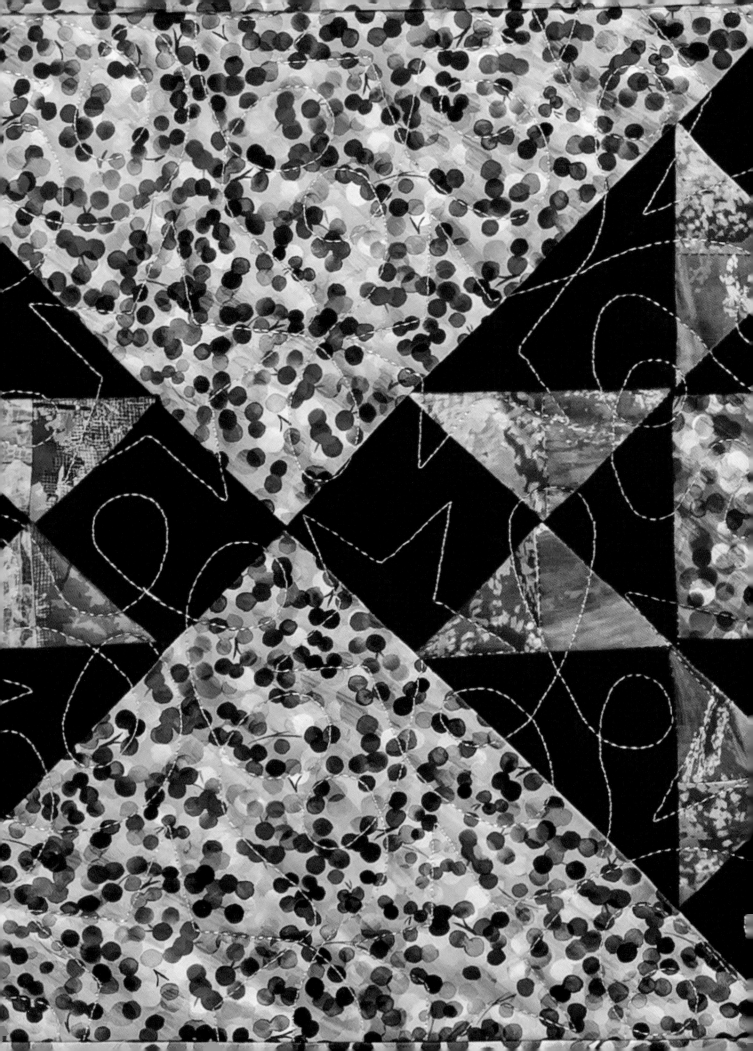

MINI MISSOURI STAR

When Missouri Star Quilt Company first began, before it even had a name, it was founded with a deep love for the "Show Me" State. Hamilton became our beloved hometown and we felt right at home among such stalwart, genuine people. This love prompted us to name our family quilting company after the place we felt the most at home. With that, we started out with our single longarm quilting machine, a name, and a dream. Big, bold, and bright, you can create your own Missouri Star table runner and turn your charm squares into the star of the show.

materials

PROJECT SIZE
43" x 18"

BLOCK SIZE
9" x 12½" unfinished,
8½" x 12" finished

PROJECT TOP
1 package of 5" print squares
  - includes cornerstones
½ yard of background fabric
  - includes sashing
1½ yards accent fabric
  - includes backing

BORDER
¼ yard

BINDING
½ yard

1 sort & cut

Select (4) 5″ print squares for the block centers and trim each to 4½″. Set the remaining print squares aside for now.

From the background fabric:

- Cut (2) 3″ strips across the width of the fabric. Subcut a **total of (16)** 3″ squares.

- Cut (2) 2½″ strips across the width of the fabric. Subcut a **total of (32)** 2½″ squares.

2 make the center squares

Draw a line once on the diagonal on the reverse side of (16) 2½″ background squares. **2A**

Lay a marked background square on 2 opposite corners of a 4½″ print square as shown, right sides together. Sew along the marked lines, then trim the excess fabric ¼″ away from the seam. **2B**

Press each snowballed corner over the seam. **2C**

Repeat to snowball the 2 remaining corners using 2 marked squares. Square to 4½″ if needed. **Make 4** center squares and set them for the moment. **2D**

2A

2B

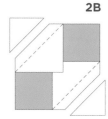

2C

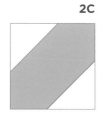

2D

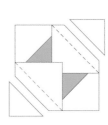
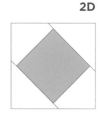

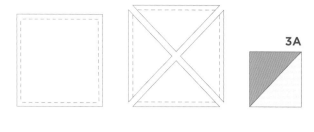

3A

3B

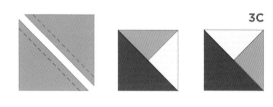

3C

3D

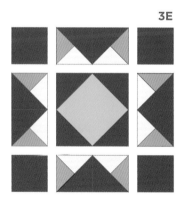

3E

3 block construction

Lay 2 unmatching 5″ print squares 1 atop of the other, right sides facing. Sew around the perimeter. Cut the sewn squares twice diagonally. Open to reveal 4 half-square triangles. Press. Do not trim. **3A**

Draw a line once on the diagonal on the reverse side of each 3″ background square. **3B**

Lay a marked square on top of a half-square triangle with the drawn line crossing over the seam of the half-square triangle. Sew ¼″ away from the drawn line on both sides. Cut on the drawn line. If you are using the trimmer, lay your unit with the quarter-triangle seam facing up. Match the centerline of the trimmer with the seam and trim each unit to 2½″, then open and press. If you are not using the slotted trimmer, open each unit and press, then measure 1¼″ from the center and trim to 2½″ square. **Make 8**. **3C**

Sew 2 units together as shown. Notice the fabric placement is reflected in both units. Press. **Make 4** star leg units. **3D**

Arrange (4) 2½″ background squares, 4 star leg units, and a center square as shown. **3E**

Sew the block together in rows. Press the top and bottom rows towards the background squares and the middle row towards the center square. Nest the seams and sew the rows together. Press. **Make 4** blocks and set any remaining 5″ print squares aside for another project. **3F**

Block Size: 8½″ unfinished, 8″ finished

3F

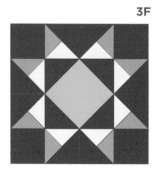

1 Lay a 2½" marked background square on 2 opposite corners of a 4½" print square as shown. Sew on the marked lines, then trim the excess fabric away and press.

2 Repeat for the 2 remaining corners. Make 4 center squares.

3 Lay 2 unmatching print squares right sides together and sew around the perimeter. Cut on both diagonals, then open and press.

4 Lay a marked 3" marked background square on a half-square triangle with the marked line crossing over the seam. Sew ¼" away from the marked line on both sides, then cut open, and press. Square each unit to 2½". Make 32.

5 Sew 2 mirrored units together as shown. Press. Make 16 star leg units.

6 Arrange (4) 2½" background squares, 4 star leg units, and a center square in 3 rows of 3 as shown. Sew the units together in rows and press in opposite directions. Nest the seams and sew the rows together.

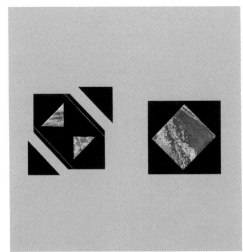

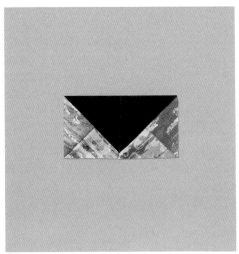

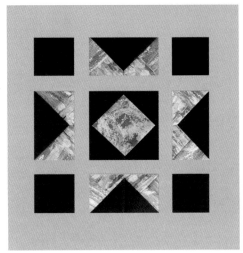

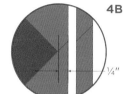

4B

¼"

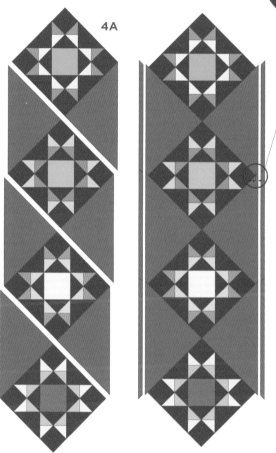

4A

4 arrange & sew

From the accent fabric, cut (1) 9½" strip across the width of the fabric. Subcut (3) 9½" squares, then cut each square once on the diagonal to yield a **total of 6** setting triangles.

Refer to diagram **4A** as necessary to lay out your blocks and setting triangles in **4 diagonal rows**. Pay close attention to the orientation of the setting triangles and sew them to the blocks to form rows. Press towards the setting triangles. Nest the rows and sew the blocks together to form the table runner top. Press.

Measure ¼" past the points of the blocks along the outer edge of the table runner and trim the setting triangles if needed. **4B**

5 quilt & bind

Layer the table runner with batting and backing, then quilt. Refer to Creating a Table Runner (pgs. 10-15) for finishing and binding instructions.

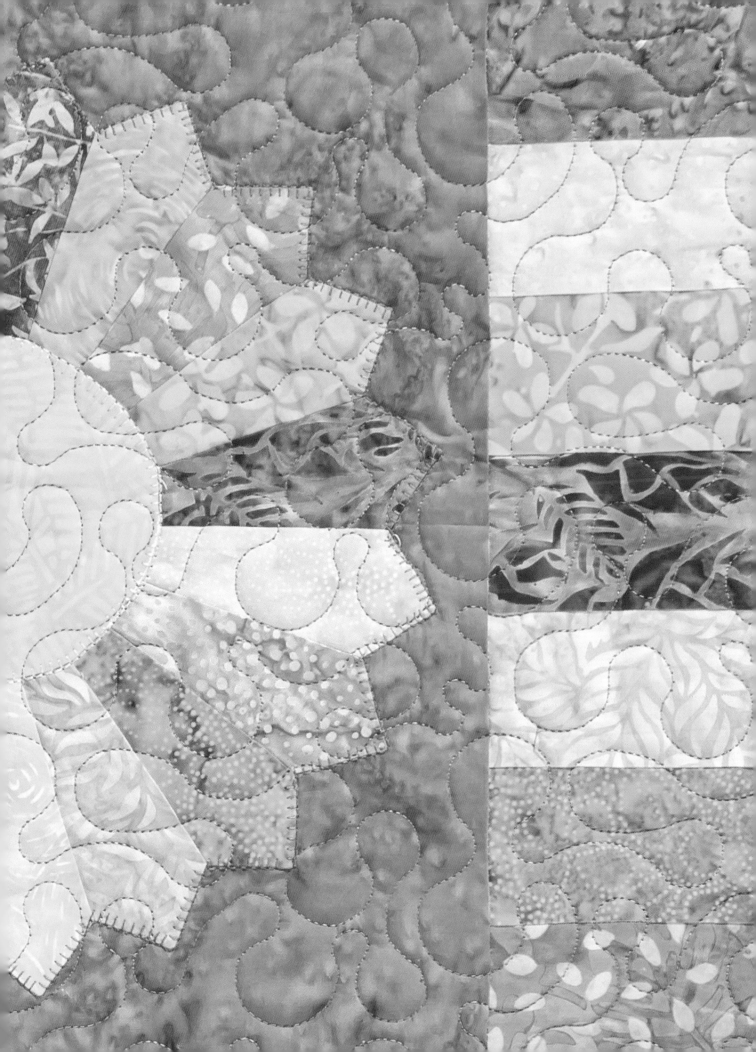

DRESDEN SUNRISE

The Dresden Plate pattern first appeared in the 1930s, and became synonymous with the pretty floral print feed sack fabrics of the time. And if you're wondering, the name "Dresden" comes from the city of the same name in Germany. This lovely place, nicknamed the "Jewel Box," was famed for its beautiful architecture and fine porcelain embellished with floral patterns. It's no wonder that the quilters of the time turned to them for inspiration! Transform your table into a colorful display with this darling Dresden table runner. Using simple techniques and easy charm packs, they come together with plenty of time to make dessert.

materials

PROJECT SIZE
37" x 14"

DRESDEN FAN BLOCK SIZE
7½" x 14½" unfinished,
7" x 14" finished

DRESDEN PLATE BLOCK SIZE
14½" unfinished, 14" finished

PROJECT TOP
1 package of 5" print squares
½ yard of background fabric

BINDING
¼ yard

BACKING
¾ yard - vertical seam(s)

OTHER
Missouri Star Large Dresden Plate
    Template for 10" Squares
¼ yard of fusible interfacing
    (20" wide)

1 cut

From the package 5″ print squares:

- Select 1 square for the Dresden plate center circle and 2 matching squares for the Dresden fan half-circles. Set these aside for section 4.

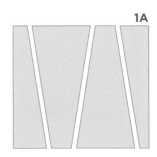

1A

- Cut 20 squares into a **total of 40** Dresden blades. Use the template to cut 2 Dresden blades per square, rotating the template 180° after the first blade is cut. **1A**

- Cut 7 squares in half to **make (14)** 5″ x 2½″ rectangles.

- Set the remaining squares aside for another project.

From the background fabric, cut (1) 14½″ strip across the width. Subcut (1) 14½″ square and (2) 14½″ x 7½″ rectangles.

From the fusible interfacing, cut (1) 5″ strip across the width. Cut (3) 5″ squares.

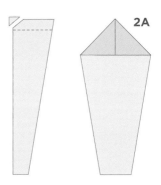

2A

2 make the blades

Fold a Dresden blade in half lengthwise, right sides facing. Sew across the wide end of the folded blade. Clip the corner and turn the blade right side out. Poke the corner out and press with the seam in the center. **Make 40** blades. **2A**

3A

3 make the fans & plate

Select 10 blades and sew them together along the long sides to form a 10 blade Dresden Fan. Press. **Make 4**. **3A**

Note: Backstitch at the outside edge of each seam.

Sew 2 of your fans together as shown to make a 20 blade Dresden Plate. **Make 1**. **3B**

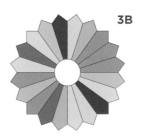

3B

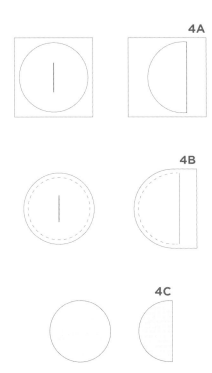

4A

4B

4C

4 make the centers

Trace a 4½″ circle and 2 half-circles on the non-adhesive side of the 3 interfacing squares. Cut a slit in the center of the drawn full circle.

Lay each marked interfacing square on a 5″ print square set aside for section 4, with the glue side of the interfacing touching the right side of the background square. **Note**: The 2 traced half-circles should be on the 2 matching 5″ print squares. Sew the pieces together by stitching on the marked circle and the curve of both half-circles. Do not sew along the straight lines of the half-circles. Trim ¼″ away from the sewn line. **4A 4B**

Turn the full sewn circle right sides out through the slit and push out the edges. Trim the 2 half-circles along the straight line then turn them right sides out and push out the edges. *Do not press*. **Make 1** center circle and **make 2** half-circles. **4C**

5 make the Dresden blocks

Lightly press the 2 background rectangles in half and then the background square in half vertically and horizontally as shown. **5A**

Using the creases as a guide, center the Dresden Fans on the rectangles along 1 long edge as shown. Center the Dresden Plate on the creased square. Pin in place. **5B**

Center a prepared half-circle on each Dresden Fan and the prepared circle on the Dresden Plate as shown. Fuse the half-circles and circle in place following the manufacturer's instructions. **5C**

Appliqué the fans, half-circles, plate, and the circle to the background using a blanket stitch or a small zigzag. **5D**

Dresden Fan Block Size:
7½″ x 14½″ unfinished, 7″ x 14″ finished

Dresden Plate Block Size:
14½″ unfinished, 14″ finished

5A

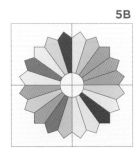

5B

1 Fold a Dresden blade in half lengthwise, right sides facing. Sew across the wide end. Clip the corner and turn the blade right side out. Poke the corner out and press. Make 40.

2 Select 10 blades and sew them together along the long sides to form a 10 blade Dresden Fan. Press. Make 4.

3 Sew 2 of your fans together as shown to make a 20 blade Dresden Plate. Make 1.

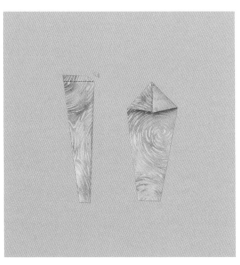

4 Lay each marked interfacing square on a 5″ print square—the glue side of the interfacing touching the right side of the background square. Stitch on the marked circle and the curve of both half-circles. Trim ¼″ away from the sewn line.

5 Turn the full sewn circle right sides out through the slit and push out the edges. Trim the 2 half-circles along the straight line then turn them right sides out and push out the edges. Do not press. Make 1 center circle and make 2 half-circles.

6 Center a prepared circle on the Dresden Plate as shown.

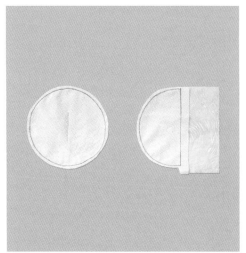

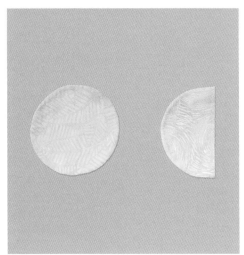

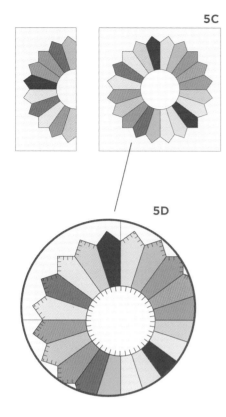

5C

5D

6 make the pieced strips

Sew (7) 2½″ x 5″ rectangles together along the 5″ sides. **Make 2** pieced strips and press. **6A**

7 arrange & sew

Arrange the Dresden Fans, pieced strips, and Dresden Plate into **1 row** as shown in the diagram below. Sew the blocks together to form a row and press towards the fans and plate blocks.

8 quilt & bind

Layer the project with batting and backing, then quilt. Refer to Creating a Table Runner (pgs. 10-15) for finishing and binding instructions.

6A

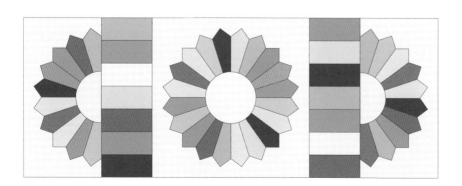

LOVE IS IN THE AIR

We know when they say "Love is in the air" we're often thinking of rom-coms and weddings. This is a sweet gift for young (or young-at-heart) love. But you know, love is in the air all the time—friends, families, sports fans, and our favorite hobbies—and especially that feeling you get when you just *know* you need to make something for someone. Show your love with this pretty heart table topper. The vines and hearts can all be applied easily with the help of your sewing machine, scissors, and a bit of fusible interfacing. Now there's no excuse not to love appliqué!

materials

PROJECT SIZE
30" x 30"

BLOCK SIZE
9½" unfinished, 9" finished

PROJECT TOP
1 package of 10" print squares
¼ yard accent fabric - includes
   sashing & inner border

OUTER BORDER
¾ yard - includes cornerstone

BINDING
½ yard

backing
1¼ yards

OTHER
Glue stick
Freezer paper

1 cut

Select 4 print squares from your package of squares and set the remaining squares aside for section 6.

Cut each selected 10″ square in half vertically and horizontally to yield 5″ squares. Keep the matching squares together.

From the background fabric cut:
- (1) 5″ strip across the width of the fabric. Subcut (8) 5″ background squares.

- (1) 2½″ strip across the width of the fabric. Subcut (16) 2½″ squares.

2 block construction

Pick up 1 set of print squares, (2) 5″ background squares, and (4) 2½″ background squares.

Draw a diagonal line on the reverse side of the 5″ background squares and 2½″ background squares. **2A**

With right sides together, place a marked 5″ square atop a 5″ print square and sew on the marked line. Trim ¼″ away from the sewn line. Repeat to make a second half-square triangle. Press the 2 seams in opposite directions. **2B 2C**

Tip: After sewing on the marked line, turn the squares and sew ½″ away from the first seam line. Cut between the 2 seam lines leaving a ¼″ seam allowance for each side. Press. Set the smaller unit aside for another project.

Place a marked 2½″ square atop the top right corner of a 5″ print square. With right sides together, sew on the marked line. Repeat with a second marked square atop the left top corner. Trim ¼″ from the sewn lines. Press. **Make 2** top units. **2D 2E**

Arrange the 2 half-square triangles and 2 top units in 2 rows as shown. Sew the units together to form the rows. Press in opposite directions. Nest the seams and sew the rows together. Press. **Make 4**. **2F**

Block Size: 9½″ unfinished, 9″ finished

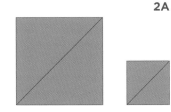

2A

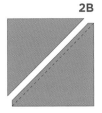

2B

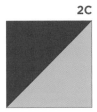

2C

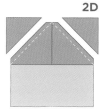

2D

2E

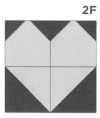

2F

3 arrange & sew

Cut (4) 1½" strips across the width of the accent fabric. Subcut 1 strip into (4) 9½" sashing rectangles. Set the remaining strips asides for the moment.

Cut a 1½" strip across the width of the outer border fabric. Subcut (1) 1½" square from the strip. Set the remainder of the strip aside for another project.

Arrange the 4 heart blocks into **2 rows of 2**. Sew the blocks on either side of a sashing rectangle. Press towards the sashing.

Sew a 9½" sashing rectangle to either side of the 1½" square to make the sashing strip. Press towards the sashing rectangles.

Sew the 2 rows together with the sashing strip between. Press.

4 inner border

Sew the (3) 1½" accent strips you set aside earlier together to make 1 long strip. Trim the borders from this strip. Measure, cut, and attach the borders to the project top. The lengths are approximately 19½" for the sides and 21½" for the top and bottom.

1 With right sides together, lay a marked background square atop a 5″ print square and sew on the marked line. Trim ¼″ from the sewn line.

2 Press. Make 2.

3 Place 2 marked 2½″ squares atop the top corners of a 5″ print square as shown. Sew on the marked line. Trim ¼″ from the sewn line.

4 Press. Make 2.

5 Lay 2 top units and 2 half-square triangles in 2 rows of 2.

6 Sew the units together to form the rows. Press in opposite directions. Nest the seams and sew the rows together. Press. Make 4.

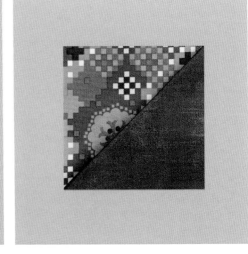

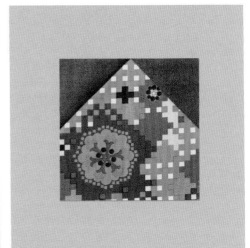

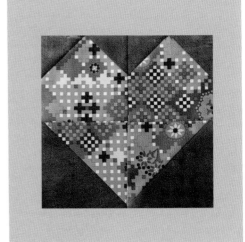

APPLIQUE HEARTS

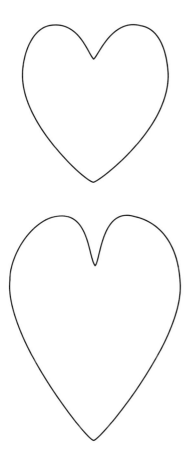

5 outer border

Cut (4) 5″ strips across the width of the background fabric. Sew the strips together to make 1 long strip. Trim the borders from this strip. Measure, cut, and attach the borders to the project top. The lengths are approximately 21½″ for the sides and 30½″ for the top and bottom.

6 appliqué

Trace 2 large and 12 small hearts onto freezer paper. Cut out and iron the shiny side to back of the scrap fabric and/or various 10″ squares. Cut the shapes out, then remove the freezer paper.

Use a glue stick to temporarily adhere the hearts to the corners of the quilt as illustrated. Use a zigzag, straight, or blanket stitch to appliqué the hearts into place.

7 quilt & bind

Layer the project with batting and backing, then quilt. Refer to Creating a Table Runner (pgs. 10-15) for finishing and binding instructions.

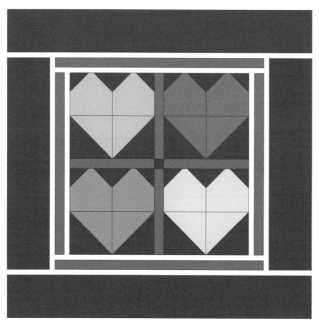

EASY CATHEDRAL WINDOW

If you've ever attempted to stitch a Cathedral quilt block together the traditional way, you know what a challenge it can be! But have no fear, our simplified method is much quicker and easier. We think you're going to love it! The timeless Cathedral Window pattern has been transformed from a tedious hand-piecing project to one that uses a sewing machine and simple charm squares. Create an elegant table topper in no time that will dazzle using this clever technique.

materials

PROJECT SIZE
27" x 18"

BLOCK SIZE
9½" unfinished, 9" finished

PROJECT TOP
1 package of 5" print squares
1 package of 5" background squares

BINDING
¼ yard

BACKING
¾ yard

1 fold & pin

Fold (32) 5″ background squares in half diagonally, wrong sides together. Press. Set the remaining squares aside for another project.

Pin 1 folded background square to a 5″ print square as shown. **Make 16** pinned units. **1A**

Pin 2 folded background squares to a 5″ print square as shown. Notice how the folded edges butt up against each other. **Make 8** pinned units. **1B**

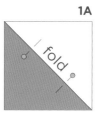

1A

1B

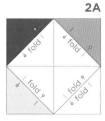

2A

2B

2 sew

Select 3 pinned units with 1 folded square and 1 pinned unit with 2 folded squares. Arrange them in 2 rows of 2 as shown. Sew the units together in pairs to form rows. Press the seams in opposite directions. Nest the seams and sew the rows together. Press. **Make 4** corner blocks. Remove any pins. **2A**

Block Size: 9½″ unfinished, 9″ finished

Select 2 pinned units with 1 folded square and 2 pinned units with 2 folded square. Arrange them in 2 rows of 2 as shown. Sew the units together as before to form an inner block. **Make 2** inner blocks. Remove any pins. **2B**

Block Size: 9½″ unfinished, 9″ finished

3 arrange & sew

Arrange the blocks in **2 rows of 3** as shown. Notice how the blocks are oriented. **3A**

Sew the blocks together to form rows. Press in opposite directions. Nest the seams and sew the rows together. Press. **3B**

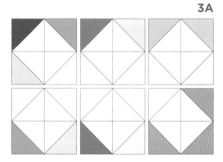

3A

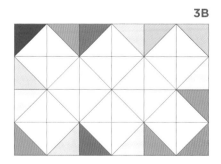

3B

1 Fold a 5″ background square once in half on the diagonal. Press to crease, then pin to the corner of a print square as shown.

2 Fold and press 2 background squares on the diagonal as before. Pin the 2 creased squares to a print square as shown.

3 Arrange 4 pinned units in 2 rows of 2 as shown.

4 Sew the pinned units together to form rows. Press. Nest the seams and sew the rows together. Press to complete a corner block. Make 4.

5 Arrange 4 pinned units in 2 rows of 2 as shown, then sew them together and press as before to create an inner block. Make 2.

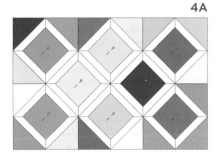

4A

4 finishing

From the backing fabric, cut (1) 22″ strip across the width of the fabric. Subcut (1) 22″ x 31″ rectangle.

Lay the backing rectangle on a flat surface, wrong side up. Place the batting rectangle and then the table runner top on top, right side up. Baste the layers together using your favorite method.

Place a 5″ print square on point over each seam line. Pin in place. **4A**

4B

Roll the pressed edges of each folded background square over each of the 5″ print squares you just placed and topstitch in place close to the pressed edge. **4B**

After you have stitched around all of the "window frames", topstitch around the perimeter using a ¼″ seam allowance. Trim all of the excess batting and backing away. Refer to Creating a Table Runner (pgs. 10-15) for binding instructions.

SUMMER NIGHTS

More than a century ago, postage stamp quilts were all the rage among quilters during the Great Depression. The idea behind these intricately-pieced quilts was saving a postage-stamp-sized scrap of every available piece of fabric you came across—from beloved items of clothing to scraps of calico feed sacks and everything in between. This pretty quilted table topper embodies the essence of the classic postage stamp quilt without all the fuss. Use our quick and easy 4-patch piecing technique with a package of charm squares, and you'll be amazed at how quickly it comes together!

materials

PROJECT SIZE
34" x 34"

PROJECT TOP
1 package 5" print squares

INNER BORDER
¼ yard

OUTER BORDER
¾ yard

BINDING
½ yard

BACKING
1¼ yards

OPTIONAL SUPPLIES
Scallops Vines & Waves Template
  by Quilt in a Day
The Bias Ruler by TQM

1 sew

Set (6) 5″ print squares aside for another project.

Layer 2 print squares together with right sides facing. Sew along 2 opposite edges using a ¼″ seam allowance. **Make 18. 1A**

Cut each sewn set of squares in half parallel to the seams at 2½″. **Note**: Measure from the outside edge of the squares rather than from the sewn seam! Open to reveal 2 charm units. Press toward the darker fabric. **Make 36. 1B**

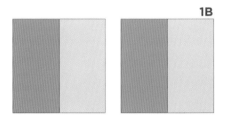

Sew the charm units together end-to-end to make a long, pieced strip. **1C**

Cut (1) 2½″ wide piece from the first charm unit and set it aside for the moment. **1D**

Fold the remaining half of the first charm unit over the next charm unit in the pieced strip. The right sides will be facing. Cut along the edge of the previously cut piece to make a 4-patch unit. Repeat, folding and cutting until you reach the end of the strip. You will have (1) 2-patch piece left at the end. Sew it to the first piece you trimmed off at the beginning. You will have a **total of (36)** 4-patch blocks. **1E 1F**

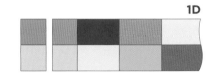

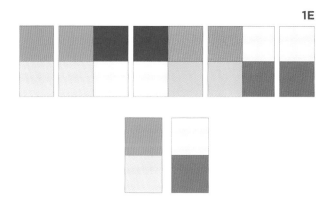

1E

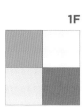

2 arrange & sew

Refer to the diagram on page 167 to arrange the 4-patch blocks in **6 rows of 6**. Sew the blocks into rows and press in opposite directions. Nest the seams and sew the rows together. Press.

3 inner border

Cut (3) 1½" strips across the width of the fabric. Sew the strips together to make 1 long strip. Trim the borders from this strip. Measure, cut, and attach the borders to the project top. The strips are approximately 24½" for the sides and 26½" for the top and bottom.

4 outer border

Cut (4) 4½" strips across the width of the fabric. Sew the strips together to make 1 long strip. Trim the borders from this strip. Measure, cut, and attach the borders to the project top. The strips are approximately 26½" for the sides and 34½" for the top and bottom.

1F

1 Layer 2 print squares together with right sides facing. Join the 2 by sewing along 2 opposite edges using a ¼" seam allowance. Cut each sewn set of square in half between the seams.

2 Open to reveal 2 charm units. Press the seam allowances toward the darker fabric.

3 Sew the charm units together end-to-end to make a long, piece strip.

4 Cut (1) 2½" wide piece from the first charm unit and set aside for the moment. Fold the remaining half of the first charm unit over the next charm unit in the strip and cut along the edge to make a 4-patch.

5 Sew the 4-patches together to make each row.

5 quilt

Layer the project with batting and backing, then quilt. After the quilting is complete, use the ruler to mark the scallops, just inside the outer edge of the project. Follow the instructions included in the booklet that came with your ruler.

6 make the bias binding

Because the edges of this project are scalloped, you will need to make bias binding. Cut the binding fabric in half to yield 2 half-yard pieces. Use the bias binding ruler and follow the manufacturer's directions to cut 2½" bias strips that total at least 156" once the strips have been sewn together. Sew the strips together in 1 long strip. Gently press the strip in half, wrong sides together. Sew the binding to the front of the project, matching the raw edges of the binding and project, and pivoting in the scallop points. Turn the folded binding edge to the back and whipstitch in place to complete your table topper. See page 47 for more great tips on how to add bias binding to pretty scalloped borders

FIND HIDDEN GOLD IN YOUR FABRIC STASH

What's the current state of your fabric stash? Are there bins buried in the depths of your garage, attic, or basement, filled with fabrics? Do you often discover fabrics in your stash that you have no memory of acquiring? We're right there with you! It's easy to store fabric, but what you actually do with it makes all the difference. It's time to start "shopping" your stash more. At the start of a new project, instead of scrambling to find the fabrics you need, imagine walking into your sewing room with confidence and feeling inspired. Let's explore how you can dig into your stash to create beautiful projects with what you have on hand.

ORGANIZE IT!

The first step to scrap busting your fabric stash is organization. It's time to pull out all those bins, boxes, and bolts from their hidey holes and put them in one big heap! Seeing all your fabric in the same place will help you get a better grip on your organizational needs and remind you of how much fabric you actually have. Take a good long afternoon or a lazy Saturday and sort through your fabrics thoughtfully. Keep the ones you love and don't be afraid to donate fabrics that don't resonate with you any longer. They aren't serving you and they could be used by someone else.

Decide what kind of organization works for you. It all depends on how you like to use your fabrics. Do you keep collections together? Or do you sort according to color? There are many ways to do it well. Keeping scrap fabrics in bins according to color helps when you want to use them later, with different subcategories like fabric weight. It's a good idea to keep quilting cottons together and heavier fabric like canvas and minky separate. As a quilter, it's important to see what you have to work with, so organizing your stash visually is key. Use your shelves for your prettiest precuts and stack them up. You might try out acrylic bolt boards or pieces of foamboard to wrap your larger pieces of fabric around. Then you can line them up on your shelf like mini bolts of fabric. They look so nice! Another option is hanging up your larger pieces of fabric in an easily accessible closet on sturdy hangers.

Next up, tackle that pile of scraps! Pick out pieces of fabric you can still fold and put them into clear bins or baskets of like colors. Fabric scraps that are too small to fold or cut into precut shapes can go into a bag to be used as stuffing for other projects like filling pincushions, pillows, pet beds, and so on. Another awesome option for scraps is making your own precuts!

MAKE YOUR OWN PRECUTS

One of the best ways to keep your scraps in check is to start cutting them down to size. Precut size, that is. When you're finished with a project and you have fabric left over, try to cut it down to either 10″ squares, 5″ squares, 2½″ squares, or 2½″ strips. Store these leftover "precuts" together by color or by theme and all of a sudden, you're ready for your next project when inspiration strikes!

FOLDING FAT QUARTERS

Any pieces of fabric that measure about 18" x 22" you can fold like a fat quarter and store them easily in a neat box or precut storage bag. Here's how we do it:

1   Iron the wrinkles out of your fat quarter.

2   Fold in half lengthwise and press (the hotdog way!).

3   Open the fold and then fold the outer edges in toward the center fold.

4   Fold the entire fat quarter in half again along the center crease.

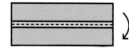

5   Fold the long strip in half and then in half again. That's it!

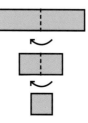

SCRAP BUSTER TABLE RUNNERS & TOPPERS

Table runners and table toppers are the perfect solution for all the different scraps you have hanging around. They easily use up 10" squares, 5" squares, and 2½" squares too. And remember, 2½" strips make awesome sashing or binding for these quick and easy projects. In this book you'll find plenty of projects that you can dip into your stash to create. Here are a few ideas just for you.

Super 2½" Strip Projects

There always seem to be plenty of strips laying around and they are so easy to use. Why not use them in a beautiful Friendship table runner? Create one for yourself and one for a friend! The Charmed Spool table runner is also perfect for your scrap strips. Line them up in pretty color combinations and you won't want to stop stitching! Find this project on page 120.

Terrific 2½″ Square Projects

Tiny squares are secretly our favorite and they are so easy to cut from scraps or leftover strips. Try them in the Mini Tumbler table runner and let your imagination run away with you! You can also give them a go in Grandma Mae's Economy Block. They look so cute all gathered together. Find this project on page 212.

Fabulous 5″ Square Projects

How cool would it be to create an entire Mini House table runner out of different fabrics? Each little house would look so unique! And here's a hint: If you have any prints featuring tiny people or animals, pop them in the doorways for even more fun. The Easy Cathedral Window table topper would absolutely shine with a wide variety of fabrics in each little fabric window. You almost can't go wrong! Find this project on page 152.

Perfect 10″ Square Projects

Mix and match fabrics in your stash to create the perfect custom look for your next project. Dresdens absolutely come alive when each blade is a different color. Go for a scrappy look and you'll be amazed at how they turn out. And the Periwinkle Table Topper can also be created from a combination of prints for a vintage look you'll adore. Find this project on page 24.

FRIENDSHIP

Remember making friendship braids and picking colors, tying knots, and watching the braids take shape? We discovered a bonus purpose for the Binding Tool - making this Friendship runner simple to piece. The binding Tool will help you cut accurate pieces from jelly roll strips to create this lovely braided look - and you get to enjoy all the fun of choosing the colors and "tying" the knots with a fun accent color. Make one for yourself and all your friends!

materials

PROJECT SIZE
15½" x 51"

BLOCK SIZE
9" x 12½" unfinished,
8½" x 12" finished

PROJECT TOP
(12) 2½" assorted print strips
1 yard solid fabric
 - includes border & binding

BACKING
1 yard - horizontal seam(s)

BINDING
½ yard

OTHER
Binding Tool by TQM

1 cut

Fold each of the (12) 2½" print strips in half. Lay the binding tool on top of a folded strip and cut. You will now have 2 braid pieces that have mirrored angles. A **total of 24** braid pieces are needed—12 pairs with mirrored angles.

From the solid fabric, cut (1) 8½" strip across the width of the fabric. Subcut (1) 8½" square from the strip, then trim the remainder into (3) 2½". From 1 of the strips, subcut a **total of (12)** 2½" squares. Set the remaining (2) 2½" strips and fabric aside for the borders and binding.

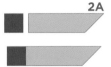

2 sew

Sew a 2½" solid square to a reversed braid piece as shown. Press. **Make 12**. **2A**

Sew a braid piece to 1 side of the 8½" solid square. Press. **2B**

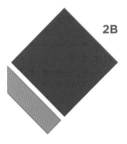

Add a reversed braid piece that has the 2½" solid square already sewn in place. Press. **2C**

Continue adding braid pieces and reversed braids in this manner until you have 6 of each sewn in place. **2D**

Repeat the previous steps for the other end of the runner.

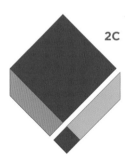

2D

3 border

From the remaining solid fabric, cut (2) 2½" strips across the width of the fabric. Cut the long straight borders from this strip.Measure, cut, and attach the borders. The strip lengths are approximately 41". Trim the shorter angled ends from the (2) 2½" strips you set aside earlier. These shorter sides are approximately 11".

Sew the 2 shorter border strips to the ends of the runner. Press. Trim the ends of the strips evenly with the edges of the main body of the runner. Repeat for the opposite end.

Add the long border strips and press. Use the short border strips as a guide to trim the ends of the longer strips. Refer to the diagram on page 179 as necessary.

1 Sew a 2½" square to a reversed braid piece.

2 Sew a braid piece to 1 side of the 8½" center square.

3 Add a reversed braid piece that has the 2½" square sewn in place.

4 Continue sewing braid pieces and reversed braid pieces until you have 6 of each sewn in place. Repeat for the other side of the runner.

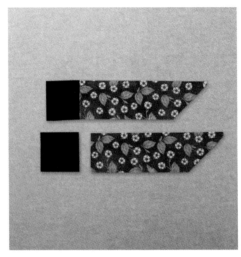

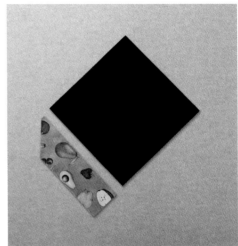

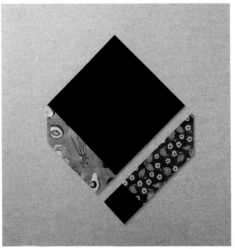

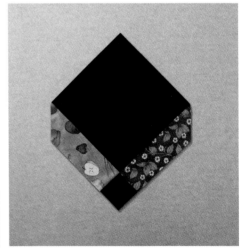

4 quilt & bind

Layer the project with batting and backing, then quilt. Refer to Creating a Table Runner (pgs. 10-15) for finishing and binding instructions.

FANCY FAN

Whenever family dinners start to become a chore, small changes can make the ordinary feel extraordinary. Getting creative with presentation or even location makes meals memorable. Simply spreading out a colorful quilt on the floor to have a picnic might encourage the pickiest eater to dig in. And macaroni and cheese tastes even better when you break out the good china, and eat by candlelight. It's all in the presentation, isn't it? If you fancy a new look for your table, pull out your trusty Dresden plate template and get stitching! Elegant fan shapes are created with Dresden blades that curve so beautifully across this timeless design.

materials

PROJECT SIZE
42" x 42"

BLOCK SIZE
10" unfinished, 9½" finished

PROJECT TOP
1 package 5" print squares
¼ yard complimentary print fabric
1½ yards background fabric
  - includes border

BINDING
½ yard

BACKING
2¾ yards - vertical seam(s)

OTHER
Missouri Star Large Dresden Plate
  Template for 10" Squares

1 cut

From the 5″ print squares, cut a **total of 80** fan blades.
Align the 5″ mark on the template with the top of a 5″
square. Cut 1 blade then flip the template 180° and cut
a second blade. Each 5″ square will yield 2 blades. **1A**

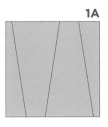

From the complimentary fabric, cut (1) 5″ strip across
the width of the fabric. Subcut (4) 5″ squares from the
strip. Use a 4¾″ circle template and cut a circle from
each of the (4) 5″ complimentary squares. Fold each
circle in half vertically and horizontally. Cut along the
fold lines to **make 16** quarter-circles. **1B**

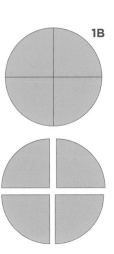

From the background fabric, cut (4) 10″ strips across the
width of the fabric. Subcut a **total of (16)** 10″ squares.
Set the remainder of the fabric aside for the border.

2 sew

Sew 5 blades together to make a fan. Press. **Make 16**. **2A**

2A

3 appliqué

Using a small blanket stitch or zigzag, appliqué a fan to 1 corner of a 10″ background square. Place a quarter-circle on the corner, covering up the raw ends of the blades. Appliqué in place to complete the block. **Make 16**. **3A**

Block Size: 10″ unfinished, 9½″ finished

4 arrange & sew

Follow the diagram on page 187 and lay out the blocks in **4 rows of 4**. Notice how the blocks are oriented.

When you are satisfied with the arrangement, sew the blocks into rows. Press the seams in opposite directions, then sew the rows together to complete the center of the quilt top. Press.

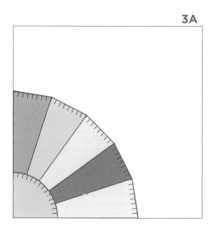

3A

1 Use a 4¾" circle template to cut a circle. Cut the circle in half vertically and horizontally to make quarter-circles.

2 Align the 5" mark of the template with the top of a 5" square. Cut 1 fan blade, then flip the ruler 180 degrees and cut another blade.

3 Sew 5 contrasting fan blades together and appliqué to 1 corner of a 10" square.

4 Place a quarter-circle on the corner, covering up the raw edges of the blades. Appliqué in place to complete the block.

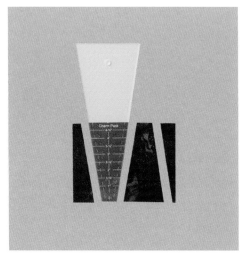

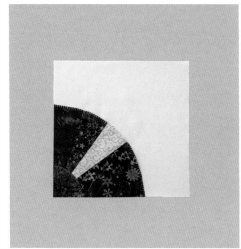

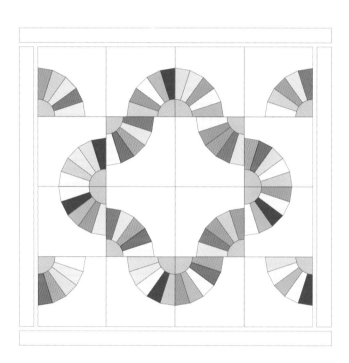

5 border

From the border fabric, cut (5) 2½" strips strips across the width of the fabric. Sew the strips together to make 1 long strip. Cut the borders from this strip. Measure, cut, and attach the borders to the project top. The strips are approximately 38½" for the sides and 42½" for the top and bottom.

6 quilt & bind

Layer the project with batting and backing, then quilt. Refer to Creating a Table Runner (pgs. 10-15) for finishing and binding instructions.

JENNY'S DOLL QUILT

When Jenny was a little girl, a kind lady at church created the sweetest doll quilt just for her. She says, "I lovingly tucked my doll beneath this tiny quilt and kissed her goodnight each day. Over the years, it has become quite worn, but I've kept it to this very day. This pretty table topper is based on that same quilt from my childhood." Now you can create the cutest table topper featuring four eight-pointed Scandinavian stars. Made with simple half-square triangles, this quick and easy project stitches up in just an afternoon.

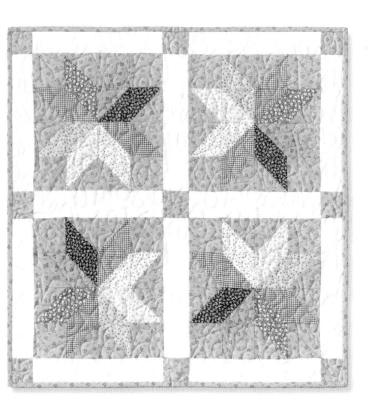

materials

PROJECT SIZE
26" x 26"

BLOCK SIZE
10½" unfinished, 10" finished

PROJECT TOP
1 package of 5" print squares
½ yard light print fabric
½ yard background fabric
  - includes cornerstones

BINDING
½ yard

BACKING
1 yard

1 cut

From the light print, cut (3) 2½" strips across the width of the fabric. Subcut a **total of (12)** 2½" x 10½" sashing rectangles.

From the background fabric, cut:

- (1) 5" strip across the width of the fabric. Subcut a **total of (8)** 5" squares.

- (2) 3" strips across the width of the fabric.
  - From 1 strip, subcut (13) 3" squares.

  - From the other strip, subcut (3) 3" squares and add them to those previously cut for a **total of 16**. Trim the strip to 2½". Subcut a **total of (9)** 2½" cornerstone squares.

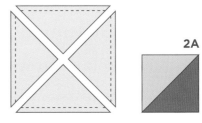

2A

2B

2 make the half-square triangles

Select 8 pairs of matching 5" print squares. Place a 5" background square atop a print square, right sides facing. Sew around the perimeter of the square ¼" from the edge. Cut the stitched squares twice on the diagonal. Open to reveal 4 matching half-square triangles. Press. Repeat, pairing a background square with a 5" print square, each time using a different print. You'll have a **total of 32** background/print half-square triangles. Square each to 3". **2A**

In the same manner, **make 4** matching half-square triangles by pairing 2 contrasting prints. Repeat, using the remaining print squares from the pairs. You will have a **total of 16** print/print half-square triangles. Square each to 3". **2B**

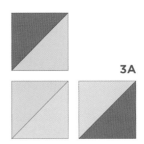

3A

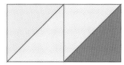

3 block construction

Lay out a print/print half-square triangle unit. Pick up print/background units that match the prints used in the first unit. Lay them out as they will be sewn together so you can keep all matching prints together. **3A**

Sew a 3″ background square to the right of the half-square triangle that is placed at the top of the print/print half-square triangle. Press. **3B**

Sew a background/print half-square triangle unit that uses a matching print to the right of the print/print half-square triangle unit as shown. Press. **3C**

Sew the 2 rows you have just made together. Press. This makes up 1 quadrant of 1 block. **Make 4** quadrants exactly alike. **3D**

Repeat to make quadrants by using matching half-square triangle units as before. You should have **4 sets of 4**. **3E**

Sew 4 quadrants together as shown to create 1 block. Press. **Make 4** blocks. **Note**: all blocks are made exactly alike. **3F**

Block Size: 10½″ unfinished, 10″ finished

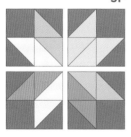

1 Lay out a print/print half-square triangle unit. Pick up print/background units that match the prints used. Lay them out as they will be sewn together so you can keep all matching prints together.

2 Place a 3″ background square next to the half-square triangle in the upper row. Sew the row together, then press.

3 Sew the 2 half-square triangles in the lower row together, then press.

4 Sew the 2 rows you have just made into a 4-patch formation.

5 Make 4 quadrants using the matching half-square triangle units as before. Repeat to make 4 sets of 4 matching quadrants.

6 Sew 4 quadrants—1 of each style—together as shown to complete the block. Make 4.

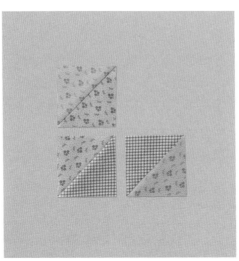
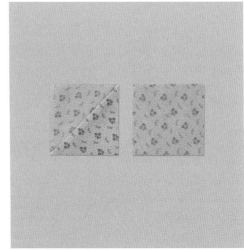
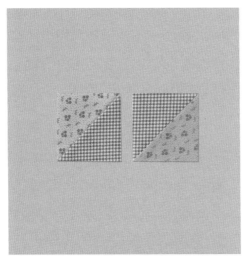
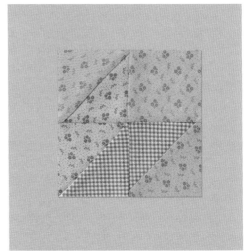
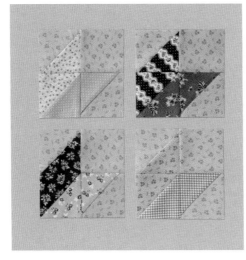
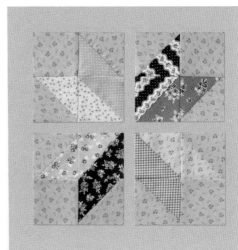

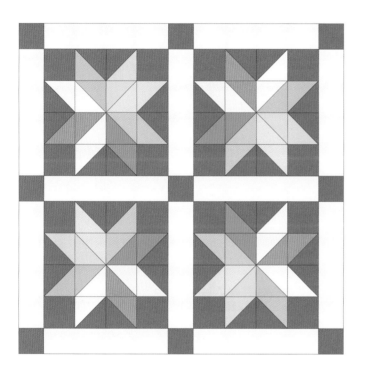

4 arrange & sew

Refer to the diagram on your left to arrange the blocks in **2 rows of 2**. Notice as the blocks are placed, each has been turned 1-quarter turn. Sew a 2½" x 10½" sashing rectangle between each block and on each end. Press towards the sashing strips.

Create 3 horizontal sashing strips by sewing a 2½" cornerstone to a sashing rectangle. Add a cornerstone, another rectangle, and end the row with a cornerstone. Press towards the sashing strips. **Make 3**.

Sew the rows and the horizontal sashing strips together to complete the project. Press.

5 quilt & bind

Layer the project with batting and backing, then quilt. Refer to Creating a Table Runner (pgs. 10-15) for finishing and binding instructions.

LEAFY TREE TOPS

Whenever we see the Sugar Maple leaves change from green to brilliant reds and even deep purple during the fall season, the urge to start sewing sets in. Midwest quilters feel this instinctively. Fall is the perfect time for "quilting season" in Missouri when the cool breezes start blowing, urging us indoors to cuddle up with a brand new project just in time for the first snowfall. Create a lovely table runner that's perfect for fall or spring, depending on your color palette. Make a couple and switch them out as the seasons change!

materials

PROJECT SIZE
24" x 54"

BLOCK SIZE
6½" unfinished, 6" finished

PROJECT TOP
1 package of 5" print squares
¾ yard background fabric
  - includes inner border

OUTER BORDER
½ yard

BINDING
½ yard

BACKING
1¾ yards

1 cut

Select (24) 5″ print squares. Cut each in half vertically and horizontally to make 2½″ squares. Each square will yield 4 squares and each block uses 4 matching squares of 1 print and 3 matching squares of a second print.

Select (4) 5″ print squares that complement the pieces you are using to make the leaves. Cut (3) 1½″ x 4″ rectangles from each square.

From 1 print square, cut (3) 1½″ squares.

Set the remaining squares aside for another project.

From the background fabric, cut:

- (2) 1½″ strips across the width of the fabric—subcut each strip into (6) 1½″ x 6½″ rectangles for a **total of 12**.

- (9) 2½″ strips across the width of the fabric. Subcut:
  - 4 strips into (16) 2½″ squares and 1 strip into (8) 2½″ squares for a **total of 72.**

  - 2 strips into (1) 2½″ x 13½″ rectangle and (1) 2½″ x 17½″ rectangles.

  - Set aside the (2) 2½″ x 17½″ rectangles, the 2 remaining strips as well as the rest of the strip from which the (8) 2½″ squares were cut. These pieces will be used when making the inner border.

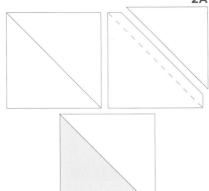

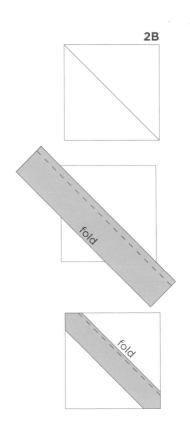

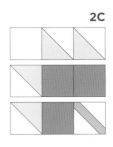

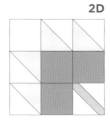

2D

3A

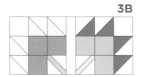

3B

3C

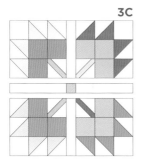

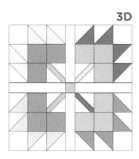

3D

2 block construction

To make the half-square triangle units, pick up 4 matching 2½″ print squares and (4) 2½″ background squares. Draw a diagonal line on the reverse side of each selected background square. Place a marked square atop a print square and sew on the marked line. Trim the excess fabric ¼″ away from the sewn seam. Press toward the darker fabric. **Make 4** and set them aside for the moment. **2A**

Choose a 1½″ x 4″ complementary rectangle and a 2½″ background square. Press the background square in half on the diagonal. Press the rectangle in half lengthwise with wrong sides facing. Open the pressed background square and align the long raw edges of the print rectangle along the crease on the right side of the background square. Stitch the rectangle to the background square using a ¼″ seam allowance. Fold the rectangle back over, covering the seam allowance and top stitch along the pressed edge. Trim the edges of the rectangle evenly with the background square to complete the stem unit. **2B**

Lay out 4 matching half-square triangle units, a stem unit, 1 background square, and (3) 2½″ print squares as shown. Sew the units together in rows. **2C**

Press the seams of the top and bottom rows to the left and the seams of the middle row to the right. Nest the seams and sew the rows together to complete the leaf block. Press. **Make 12**. **2D**

Block Size: 6½″ unfinished, 6″ finished

1 Draw a diagonal line once on the reverse side of the 2½" background squares. Place a marked square atop a print square and sew on the line. Trim the excess fabric ¼" away from the sewn seam. Press. Make 4

2 Press a 2½" background square once on the diagonal. Press a 1½" x 4" complementary rectangle once in half lengthwise, wrong sides together. Align the raw edges of the rectangle crease of the square, then stitch in place. Flip the rectangle over the seam, then topstitch along the pressed edge.

3 Sew 2 matching half-square triangle units to a 2½" background square to make the top row. Sew a half-square triangle unit to (2) 2½" matching print squares to make the center row. Sew a half-square triangle to a 2½" square. Add a stem unit to complete the bottom row.

4 Sew the 3 rows together to complete the block.

5 Select 4 blocks. Sew 1 to either side of a 1½" x 6½" background rectangle. Make 2 rows in this manner as shown. Sew a 1½" x 6½" background rectangle to either side of a 1½" square. Sew the 3 rows together.

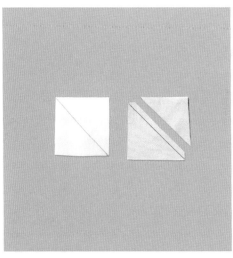

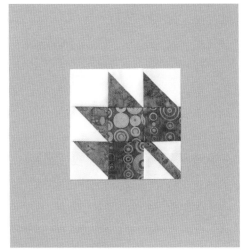

3 arrange & sew

Make a pieced sashing strip by sewing a 1½″ x 6½″ background rectangle to each side of a 1½″ print square. Press the seams toward the 1½″ square. **Make 3**. **3A**

Sew a leaf block to both sides of a 1½″ x 6½″ background rectangle. Press the seams toward the rectangle. **Make 6** leaf units. **3B**

Sew a leaf unit to each side of a pieced sashing strip. **Make 3** large leaf units. **3C 3D**

Refer to the diagram on your left to arrange the large leaf units as shown with a 2½″ x 13½″ sashing strip between each unit. Sew the units together in 1 virtical row and press toward the sashing.

4 inner border

Pick up the background pieces that were set aside earlier for the inner border. Set aside the (2) 2½″ x 17½″ rectangles for the moment. Sew the remaining strips together to make 1 long strip. Measure, cut, and attach the borders to the project top. The strips are approximately 43½″. Add a 2½″ x 17½″ rectangle to each shorter end.

5 outer border

Cut (4) 4″ strips across the width of the fabric. Sew the strips together to make 1 long strip. Trim the borders from this strip. Measure, cut, and attach the borders to the project top. The strips are approximately 47½″ for the sides and 24½″ for each end.

6 quilt & bind

Layer the project with batting and backing, then quilt. Refer to Creating a Table Runner (pgs. 10-15) for finishing and binding instructions.

TROPICAL PARADISE

Did you know that the pineapple is a symbol of hospitality? You'll find it in luxurious hotels and modest motels, too, welcoming guests to rest, relax, and enjoy their stay. The delicious, tropical treat is bright and inviting. These pretty patchwork pineapples are bright and cheerful, too. Don't let the curves fool you, they're simple to piece together and make a lovely table or counter that much more welcoming.

materials

PROJECT SIZE
52" x 20"

BLOCK SIZE
16½" unfinished, 16" finished

PROJECT TOP
(11) 5" squares of orange fabric
¼ yard of green fabric
1 yard of background fabric

BORDER
½ yard

BINDING
½ yard

BACKING
1¾ yards

OTHER
Missouri Star Drunkard's Path
   Circle Templates Set – Small
Clearly Perfect Slotted Trimmer
   A - optional

1 cut

From the green fabric, cut (1) 5" strip across the width of the fabric. Subcut a **total of (8)** 5" squares.

From the background fabric, cut:

- (3) 8½" strips across the width of the fabric. Subcut a **total of (9)** 8½" squares.

- (1) 4½" strip across the width of the fabric. Subcut a **total of (9)** 4½" squares.

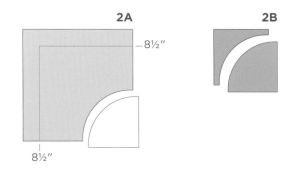

2 make the pineapple bodies

Cut

Lay an 8½" background square on your cutting surface. Line up the 8½" marks on the Drunkard's Path template A with your square and carefully cut along the curve. Repeat to cut a **total of 9** background A pieces. Set the quarter-circle pieces aside for another project. **2A**

Lay a 5" yellow square on your cutting surface. Place the Drunkard's Path template B in the corner of your square as shown. Cut along the curve. Repeat to cut a **total of 9** yellow B pieces. **2B**

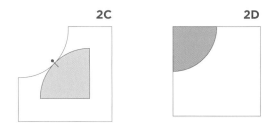

Unit Assembly

Pair an A piece with a B piece. Fold each piece in half on the diagonal and finger press to mark the midway point of each curved edge. Place the B piece on top of the A piece, right sides facing, and finger pressed centers aligned. Pin at the midway point and at both ends of the seam allowance. **Note**: Add more pins as needed. **2C**

Stitch the 2 pieces together along the curve. Use your fingers to ease in the fullness around the curve and avoid stretching the fabric as you sew. Press towards the A piece to complete the unit. **Make 9**. **2D**

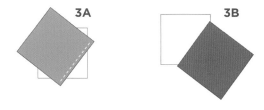

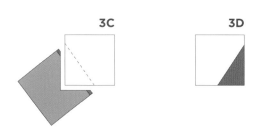

3 make the pineapple crowns

Wonky Points

Place a 5″ green square on an angle (any angle) atop a 4½″ background square, right sides facing, as shown. Make sure your green square is placed a little past the halfway point. Sew ¼″ in from the angled edge of the green square. **3A**

Press the piece flat to set the seam, then press the green piece over the seam allowance. **3B**

Turn the unit over and use the background square as a guide to trim the green fabric so that all of the edges are even. Save the trimmed scrap for the next wonky point. (You should be able to make at least 2 wonky points from each green square.) **3C 3D**

Note: If you wish to trim the excess background fabric from the back of the unit, you can turn the unit right side up, fold the green fabric of the wonky points back, and trim the excess background fabric ¼″ away from the sewn seam. Fold the wonky points back so the right side of the fabric is facing up and press.

Place the trimmed green scrap on the adjacent side of the square. Make sure the edge of the green piece crosses over the first wonky point by at least ¼″. Stitch ¼″ in from the edge of the green piece. **3E**

Press to set the seam, then press the green piece over the seam allowance. Turn the unit over and use the background square as a guide to trim the green fabric so all of the edges are even. Notice your square is still 4½″. **Make 6** wonky point units. **Tip**: Have fun with this and don't try to make all of the units alike! **3F 3G**

Half-Square Triangles

Mark a diagonal line on the reverse side of each remaining 5″ yellow square. **3H**

Place a marked square atop a 5″ green square with right sides facing. Sew on both sides of the marked line using a ¼″ seam allowance. Cut on the marked line. Use the slotted trimmer to square each unit to 4½″ then press open—or press, then square to 4½″ if you're not using the trimmer. You'll **make 4** half-square triangles—set 1 aside for another project. **3I**

Unit Assembly

Arrange 2 wonky point units, 1 half-square triangle, and (1) 4½″ background square as shown. Sew the unit together in 2 rows. Press the rows in opposite directions. Nest the seams and sew the rows together to complete the unit. **Make 3**. **3J 3K**

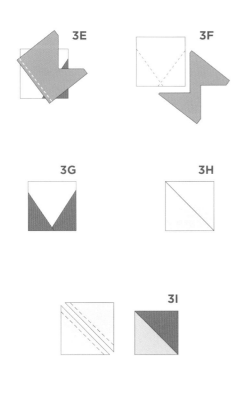

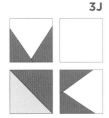

1 Lay an 8½" background square on your cutting surface. Line up the 8½" marks on the Drunkard's Path template A with and cut along the curve. Lay a 5" yellow square on your cutting surface. Place the Drunkard's Path template B in the corner of your square as shown. Cut along the curve.

 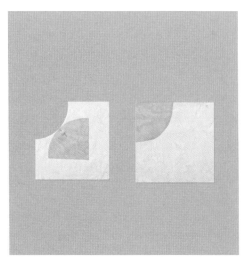

2 Place the B piece on top of the A piece, right sides facing, and finger pressed centers aligned. Pin. Stitch together along the curve. Press towards the A piece to complete the unit.

3 Place a 5" green square on an angle atop a 4½" background square, right sides facing. Sew ¼" in from the angled edge of the ombre square. Press the green piece over the seam allowance.

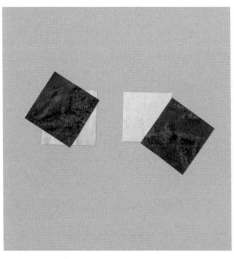 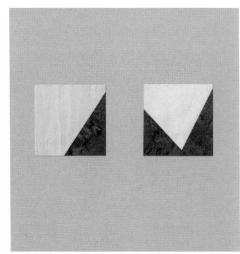

4 Turn the unit over and use the background square as a guide to trim the green ombre fabric so that all of the edges are even. Repeat to add another wonky point to the opposite edge and trim.

5 Mark a diagonal line once on the reverse side of each 5" yellow square. Place a marked square atop a 5" green square with right sides facing. Sew on both sides of the marked line using a ¼" seam allowance. Cut on the marked line. Square each unit to 4½".

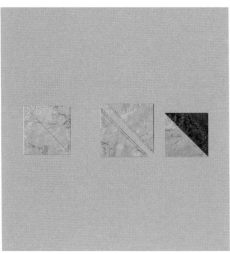 

6 Arrange 3 pineapple body units and 1 pineapple crown unit as shown. Sew the block together in 2 rows. Press. Nest the seams and sew the rows together. Press.

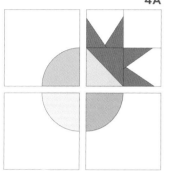
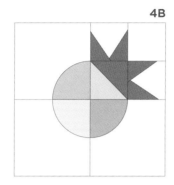

4 block construction

Arrange 3 pineapple body units and 1 pineapple crown unit as shown. Sew the block together in 2 rows. Press the rows in opposite directions. Nest the seams and sew the rows together. Press. **Make 3**. **4A 4B**

Block Size: 16½" unfinished, 16" finished

5 arrange & sew

Arrange the blocks into **1 row of 3** as shown in the diagram on your left. Sew the blocks together to form rows and press in opposite directions. Nest the seams and sew the rows together. Press.

6 border

From the border fabric, cut (4) 2½" strips across the width of the fabric. Sew the strips together to create 1 long strip. Trim the borders from this strip. Measure, cut, and attach the borders to the project top. The strip lengths are approximately 16½" for the sides and 52½" for the top and bottom.

7 quilt & bind

Layer the project with batting and backing, then quilt. Refer to Creating a Table Runner (pgs. 10-15) for finishing and binding instructions.

GRANDMA MAE'S ECONOMY BLOCK

Creating quilt blocks that use fabric well is something we enjoy doing because we hate to see good fabric go to waste. The vintage Economy Block is aptly-named, from a time when carefully placing fabric to use every scrap built these beautiful intricate-looking quilts. Staggering the rows adds a total wow to this runner, setting all the blocks on point and making a small slice to straighten up the edges. Now you can try them in a table runner that's definitely granny-approved.

materials

PROJECT SIZE
66½" x 19"

BLOCK SIZE
7¼" unfinished, 6¾" finished

PROJECT TOP
1 roll of 2½" print strips
2 packages of 5" background squares

BINDING
½ yard

BACKING
1½ yards - vertical seam(s)

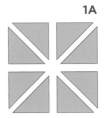

1A

1 sort & cut

From the roll of 2½" print strips, select 15 strips and set the remaining strips aside for another project.

Fold each of the selected 2½" print strips into fourths. Cut (2) 2½" squares and (1) 2½" x 3½" rectangle from each folded strip. Subcut the 2½" x 3½" rectangles in half to yield 1¼" x 3½" rectangles. Keep the (8) 2½" squares and (8) 1¼" x 3½" rectangles from each strip together as a set. **Make 15** sets.

2A

Select (60) 5" background squares from your packages of squares.
- Cut (4) 1¼" strips across the width of (2) 5" squares, then subcut a **total of (29)** 1¼" squares.

2B

- Cut (58) 5" squares in half vertically and horizontally and then along both diagonals to yield a **total of 464** setting triangles. **1A**

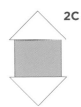

2C

2D

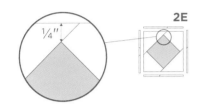

2E

¼"

2F   **2G**

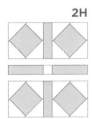   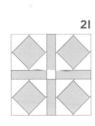

2H   **2I**

2 make blocks

Select 32 setting triangles, (2) 1¼" background squares, and 1 set of print pieces. This will be enough to **make 2** identical blocks.

Tip: Chain piecing makes this project a breeze! If you are comfortable, continue sewing for a few stitches after you've reached the end of the fabric and then slide the next unit under your presser foot without breaking the thread.

Center the long edge of a setting triangle along 1 side of each 2½" print square from your set. Sew along the matched edges. **2A**

Clip threads between the units if you like. Place another setting triangle on the opposite side of each square. Sew along the matched edges. Clip the threads between the units, then open and press towards the triangles. **2B 2C**

Repeat to add setting triangles to the remaining sides of each of the print squares in your set. **2D**

Make sure there is ¼" left outside of each point and square each unit to 3½". **2E**

Note: You can make 4 rows in the next step to make 2 identical blocks at the same time.

Sew a 1¼" x 3½" print rectangle between 2 units you just made as shown. Press towards the rectangle. **Make 2** rows for each block. **2F**

Sew a 1¼" background square between (2) 1¼" x 3½" print rectangles. Press towards the rectangles. **Make 2**. **2G**

Arrange the 3 rows you have created as shown. Nest the seams and sew the rows together. Press. **Make 29** blocks. **2H 2I**

Block Size: 7¼" unfinished, 6¾" finished

1 Cut a 5″ square in half vertically and horizontally and then along both diagonals to make 8 setting triangles.

2 Using a ¼″ seam allowance, sew 2 setting triangles on opposite sides of a 2½″ print square. Press.

3 Repeat with an additional 2 setting triangles and sew them on the 2 remaining sides of the print square. Press. Make sure there is ¼″ left outside of each point and square unit to 3½″. Make 4.

4 Sew 2 units to either side of a sashing rectangle. Make 2. Sew 2 sashing rectangles to either side of a 1½″ background square. Press towards the sashing rectangles.

5 Arrange the 3 rows as shown.

6 Sew the rows together and press. Make 29 blocks.

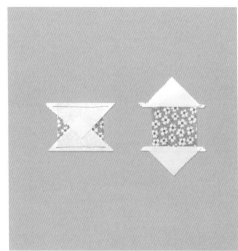
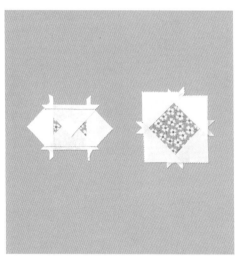

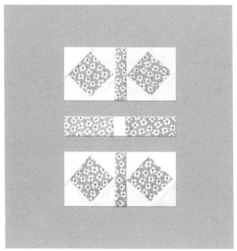
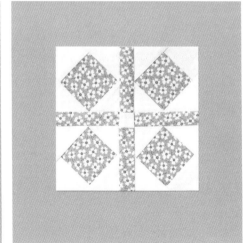

3A

3 arrange & sew

Arrange your blocks in **7 diagonal rows** as shown.
Sew the blocks in diagonal rows and press in opposite
directions. Nest the seams and sew the rows together.
Press. **3A**

Trim the top and bottom to make the edges straight,
leaving a ¼″ seam allowance. **3B**

4 quilt & bind

Layer the project with batting and backing, then quilt.
Refer to Creating a Table Runner (pgs. 10-15) for
finishing and binding instructions.

3B

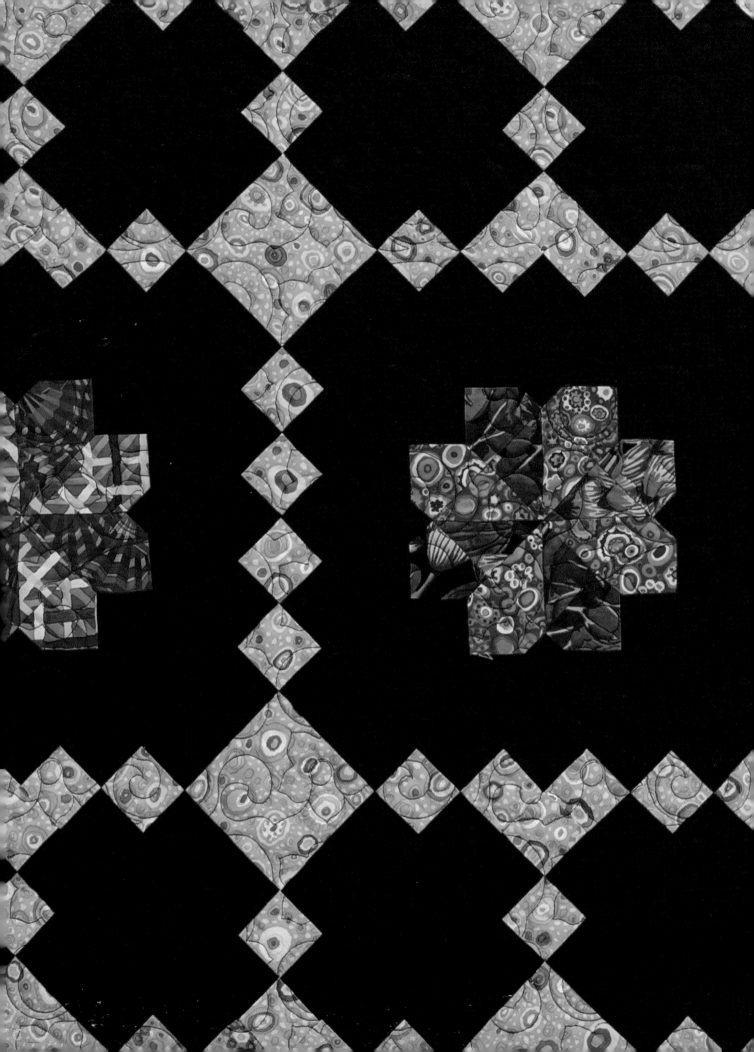

FLOWER CHAIN

Quilters make great gardeners. The act of sowing a seed and having the hope that it will grow and produce fruit incites creativity just as much as making a stitch and imaging a beautiful quilt when you're all through. Each process is magical and seeing plants start to grow is as satisfying as stitching together seams that nest perfectly. There's no better way to remember that we literally reap what we sow. How does your garden grow? Stitch it up and soon you'll see! Create a quaint quilted table runner filled with blooming pinwheel flowers featuring petite eight-pointed petals, all accented with lovely Irish Chain blocks.

materials

TABLE RUNNER SIZE
67½" x 27"

BLOCK SIZE
10" unfinished, 9½" finished

PROJECT TOP
1 package of 5" print squares*
1¼ yards accent fabric
2¼ yards background fabric

BINDING
½ yard

BACKING
2 yards

OPTIONAL
Clearly Perfect Slotted Trimmer A
Missouri Star 10" Square Template

*If you'd like, you may substitute
8 pairs of 5" print squares for the
package of squares.*

1 cut

Select 8 pairs of 5″ print squares and set the remaining squares aside for another project.

From the accent fabric, cut (3) 4″ strips and (12) 2″ strips across the width of the fabric.

From the background fabric, cut:

- (3) 7″ strips across the width of the fabric.

- (3) 4″ strips across the width of the fabric.

- (1) 2½″ strip across the width of the fabric. Subcut a **total of (16)** 2½″ squares.

- (14) 2″ strips across the width of the fabric. Subcut 8 strips into a **total of (48)** 2″ x 7″ rectangles. Set the remaining 6 strips aside for the moment.

- (3) 1¾″ strips across the width of the fabric. Subcut a **total of (64)** 1¾″ squares.

- (4) 1½″ strips across the width of the fabric. Subcut (2) 1½″ x 10½″ rectangles and (2) 1½″ x 8½″ rectangles from each strip for a **total of 8** of each size.

2 make the chain blocks

Sew a 2″ background strip to the top and bottom of a 4″ accent strip. Press towards the darker fabric. **Make 3**. Cut these strip sets into 4″ increments to create a **total of 24** A units. **2A**

Sew a 2″ accent strip to the top and bottom of a 4″ background strip. Press towards the darker fabric. **Make 3**. Cut these strip sets into 2″ increments to create a **total of 48** B units. **2B**

Sew a 2″ accent strip to the top and bottom of a 7″ background strip. Press the seams toward the darker fabric. **Make 3**. Cut these strip sets into 2″ increments to create a **total of 48** C units. **2C**

2A

2B

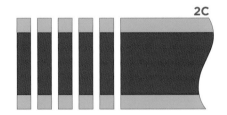

2C

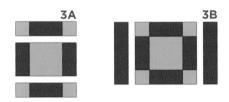

3A

3B

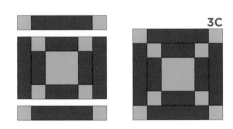

3C

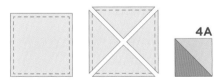

4A

3 chain block construction

Lay 1 A unit and 2 B units in 3 rows as shown. Nest the seams and sew the rows together to complete a block center. Press. **3A**

Sew a 2″ x 7″ background rectangle to either side of the block center. Press the seams toward the outside edges. **3B**

Sew a C unit to the top and bottom of the center unit, nesting the seams as you go. Press. **Make 24**. **3C**

Block Size: 10″ unfinished, 9½″ finished

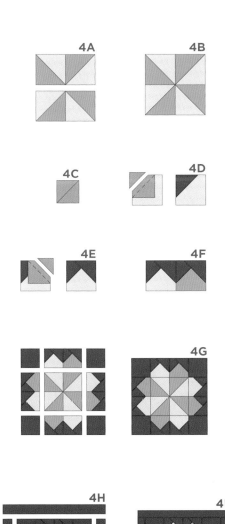

4 flower block construction

Select 2 different pairs of 5″ print squares. Lay 2 unmatching 5″ print squares together, right sides facing. Sew around the perimeter. Cut the sewn squares twice diagonally. Use trimmer A to square each unit to 2½″ then press open—or press, then square to 2½″ if you're not using the trimmer. Each set of sewn squares will yield 4 half-square triangles. **4A**

Arrange the 4 half-square triangles in a pinwheel as shown. Sew the units together in 2 rows and press in opposite directions. Sew the rows together, then press to complete the pinwheel. **4B**

Cut the other 2 selected 5″ print squares in half vertically and horizontally to create (4) 2½″ squares of each print.

Mark a diagonal line once on the reverse side of each 1¾″ background square. **4C**

Place a marked square on 1 corner of a 2½″ print square, right sides facing. Sew on the marked line. Trim the excess fabric away ¼″ from the sewn seam. Press open. **4D**

Repeat with another 1¾″ marked background square to snowball an adjacent corner. Snowball 2 adjacent corners of each of the 2½″ print squares to **make 2** *sets* of 4 matching petals. **4E**

Sew a petal of each print side by side as shown. Press. **Note**: Reference **4G** as needed to make sure that the order of the prints in your petals will match the pinwheel. **Make 4** petal units. **4F**

Arrange (4) 2½″ background squares, 4 petal units, and the pinwheel in 3 rows of 3 as shown. Sew the units together in rows and press in opposite directions. Nest the seams and sew the rows together. Press. **4G**

Sew a 1½″ x 8½″ background rectangle to either side of the unit you just made. Press towards the rectangles. Sew a 1½″ x 10½″ background rectangle to the top and bottom of the unit. Press towards the rectangles. Use the square template and align the centerline with the center seams or measure 5″ from the center seams and trim the block to 10″ square. **Make 4**. **4H 4I**

Block Size: 10″ unfinished, 9½″ finished

1 Lay 1 A unit and 2 B units in 3 rows as shown. Nest the seams and sew the rows together to complete the block center. Sew a 2″ x 7″ background rectangle to either side of the block center. Press the seams toward the outside edges.

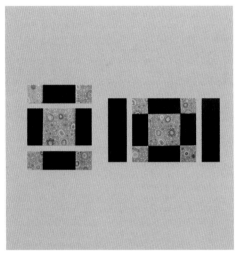
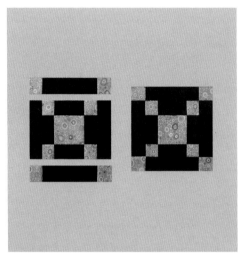

2 Sew a C unit to the top and bottom of the center unit, nesting the seams as you go. Press. Make 24.

3 Lay 2 unmatching 5″ print squares together, right sides facing. Sew around the perimeter. Cut the sewn squares twice diagonally. Square each unit to 2½″. Each set of sewn squares will yield 4 half-square triangles.

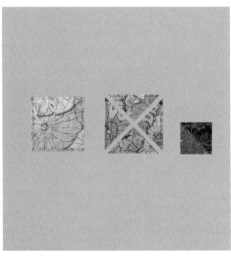

4 Arrange the 4 half-square triangles in a pinwheel as shown. Sew the units together in 2 rows and press in opposite directions. Sew the rows together, then press to complete the pinwheel.

5 Place a marked square atop the top right corner of a 2½″ print square. Sew on the marked line. Trim ¼″ from the sewn line. Press. Repeat to add a second marked square on the top left corner. Press. Make 2 sets of 4 matching petals. Sew a petal of each print side by side.

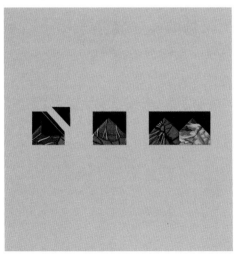

6 Arrange (4) 2½″ background squares, 4 petal units, and the pinwheel in 3 rows of 3 as shown. Sew the units together in rows and press in opposite directions. Nest the seams and sew the rows together. Press. Make 4.

5A

5 arrange & sew

Refer to the diagram to lay out your blocks in **8 diagonal rows**. The first and last row each consists of 1 chain block. The second and seventh row each consist of 3 chain blocks. Rows 3 through 7 start and end with 2 chain blocks with a flower block in the center. **5A**

Once you are happy with your layout, sew the blocks together in diagonal rows. Press the rows in opposite directions. Nest the seams and sew the rows together. Press.

5B

Trim the sides, top, and bottom to make the edges straight, leaving a ¼″ seam allowance beyond the outer print diamonds. **5B**

6 quilt & bind

Layer the project with batting and backing, then quilt. Refer to Creating a Table Runner (pgs. 10-15) for finishing and binding instructions.

ACKNOWLEDGEMENTS

Creating this book has been a pleasure with the help of such an incredible team of over twenty talented people. It seems to come together like magic and I can hardly believe it when I hold the finished book in my hands, but please know that there is a vast amount of work happening behind the scenes that readers will never see. I want each and every member of the Missouri Star Publishing Team to know how valued they are. What we are able to make together is absolutely incredible. Thank you for your hard work and imagination. You help bring these projects to life!

The Publishing Team is honestly a dream team and I want to thank my daughter, Natalie, for all the wonderful work she does as the Executive Editor. She's always been my right-hand girl since she was little. Her creativity constantly astounds me. I want to thank my sweet daughter-in-law, Misty, for her support and inventiveness with all these fun projects. It's been a joy to see her grow into the quilter she is today.

I want to thank our stalwart Creative Director, Christine Ricks, for her extraordinary efforts to make this book both beautiful and useful. And I also want to thank our newest designer, Grant Flook, for his fresh perspective on this book. It is breathtaking!

Thank you sincerely to our tireless pattern writers, Jessica Toye, Kimberly Forman, and Denise Lane, who take our designs and create detailed patterns to complete them. You make it seem easy and that speaks volumes! A big thank you goes out to our clever sewists, Courtenay Hughes, Carol Henderson, Janice Richardson, and my personal assistant, Cathleen Tripp, who have beautifully remade projects especially for this book. You are miraculous and you teach me new things all the time.

I want to thank our lead writer, Nichole Spravzoff, who always makes me sound good and creates well-written articles to go along with these patterns. And I also want to thank Liz Gubernatis who has been instrumental in guiding the content of this book to bring in even more of what makes Missouri Star special.

I am so grateful to our photographers, Mike Brunner, Lauren Dorton, as well as the Derek Israelsen Studio, and our stylist, Jennifer Dowling, who take gorgeous photographs with great care to help illustrate this book. A sincere thank you to our photo editor, Dustin Weant, is needed as well. He makes all the images truly shine! And last, but not least, I want to thank our printing coordinator, Rob Stoebener, who handles all the deadlines and makes sure this book gets to you on time!

Finally, I want to thank you, our dedicated readers. We couldn't do any of this without your continued support and love for quilting! Keep on stitching with all your heart and sharing your creativity with the world. Your efforts really do make a difference.

Jenny

26 - PERIWINKLE

Lady Bird by Crystal Manning for Moda Fabrics

32 - HARD CANDY

Hugs and Kisses by Studio Fabrics

38 - FLIRTY

Paintbox Solids by Elizabeth Hartman for Robert Kaufman

50 - BORDERING TRIANGLE

Blossom Batiks Splash by Flaurie & Finch for RJR Fabrics

56 - CANDY TWIST

Hopscotch Candy Necklace by Jamie Fingal for RJR Fabrics

64 - PONY EXPRESS

Chicken Scratch by Kaye Englewood for Wilmington Prints

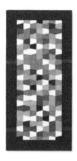

72 - MINI TUMBLER

Bee Cross Stitch by Lori Holt for Riley Blake

78 - FLICKERING STARLIGHT

Kona Cotton Solids by Robert Kaufman Fabrics

86 - HEXAGON BRAID

Saguaro by Christina Camelli for Maywood Studio

94 - FLOWER FANCY

Mirabelle by Fig Tree & Co. for Moda Fabrics

102 - MINI HOUSE

Jungle Paradise by Stacy Iest Hsu for Moda Fabrics

112 - DRESDEN SUNBURST

Let Freedom Ring by Nancy Gere for Windham Fabrics

120 - CHARMED SPOOLS

Gelato Ombre by Maywood Studio

128 - MINI MISSOURI STAR

Nature's Pace by Studio RK for Robert Kaufman Fabrics

136 - DRESDEN SUNRISE

Tropicana Twist Batiks by Kathy Engle for Island Batik

144 - LOVE IS IN THE AIR

Love Always, AM by Anna Maria Horner for Free Spirit Fabrics

152 - EASY CATHEDRAL WINDOW

Prairie by Corey Yoder for Moda

160 - SUMMER NIGHTS

Belcourt by Studio RK for Robert Kaufman

172 - FRIENDSHIP

From the Farm by Kris Lammers for Maywood Studio

180 - FANCY FAN

Very Merry by Kathy Engle for Island Batik

188 - JENNY'S DOLL QUILT

Sugar Sack by Whistler Studios for Windham Fabrics

196 - LEAFY TREE TOPS

Artisan Batiks Round and Around by Lunn Studios for Robert Kaufman Fabrics

204 - TROPICAL PARADISE

Opulent Orange Batik Solids by Kathy Engle for Island Batik

REFERENCE - *Articles*